The
Myth of Red Texas

Nation Books

Nation Books is a collaboration between *The Nation* magazine and OR Books.

The Nation was founded by abolitionists in 1865 and still appears monthly in print and online at thenation.com.

OR Books is a publishing company that embraces progressive change in politics, culture, and the way we do business. Find out more at orbooks.com.

Also available from Nation Books

The Nine Have Spoken
The Nation vs. the Supreme Court, 1870 to Today
Edited by Richard Kreitner

American Carnage
How Trump, Musk, and DOGE Butchered the US Government
By Sasha Abramsky

Forthcoming in this series

Obsolete
Power, Profit, And The Race For Machine Superintelligence
By Garrison Lovely

The Great Betrayal
How the Democrats Became the Party of War
By James Carden

Against Black Nationalism
From Pan-Africanism to the New Deal
By Paul Prescod

In blood-red states such as Texas, politics operates under the fallacy that these places were always conservative, and it would be foolish, even utopian, to propose a progressive alternative. *The Myth of Red Texas*, David Griscom's debut book, reassesses this misconception, arguing that the Lone Star Left must embrace its hidden past to reach a brighter future.

Cowboys on strike, socialists on the ballot, farmers fighting tooth and claw for what they termed the "cooperative commonwealth"—Texas was once a wellspring of radicals hell-bent on taking power from the robber barons who ruled the day.

With a careful eye for history, Griscom demonstrates how Texans' left-wing parties, from the populists to the socialists, organized against the Right and often won—and how reclaiming that tradition can help today's Left break the political deadlock in Texas and beyond.

The
Myth of Red Texas

Cowboys, Populism, and
Class War in the Radical South

David Griscom

Nation Books

Published in association with OR Books

Published by *The Nation,* in collaboration with
OR Books, New York and London

Visit our website at www.orbooks.com

All rights information: rights@orbooks.com

First printing 2026

The manufacturer's authorised representative in the EU for product
safety is Authorised Rep Compliance Ltd, 71 Lower Baggot Street,
Dublin D02 P593 Ireland (www.arccompliance.com)

Typeset by Lapiz Digital. Printed by BookMobile, USA, and CPI, UK.

Cover photo: *A group of Texas cowboys*, ca. 1901 © Detroit Publishing
Co./William Henry Jackson. Retrieved from the Library of Congress

OR Books,
40 Loisaida Avenue,
New York, NY 10009

paperback ISBN 978-1-68219-645-8 • ebook ISBN 978-1-68219-646-5

Table of Contents

Acknowledgments

This project has been an exciting undertaking, but like any effort, it was not done alone. A special thanks to Matt Lech, my co-host on Left Reckoning, for shouldering extra responsibility when needed, listening to me ramble about cattle brands and Old West lore, and providing much-needed insight. This book would not have been possible without the incisive and thoughtful edits by my editor, Sam Russek. To my late and good friend Michael Brooks, thank you for taking me under your wing years ago, which opened doors I never could have opened on my own. Among the many things I'm sad I was never able to share with you, I am deeply saddened that I never got to take you around Texas; it's especially difficult knowing we were mere days away from that being a possibility. I have only come around recently to agreeing with your strongly held belief that you would have been able to pull off a Stetson. To Bita, Charles, and Mazdak, thank you for welcoming me into your family. To my mother Cassie, my sister Abbey, and my brother Nicolas, thank you for giving me guidance, confidence, and friendship throughout my life. To my darling wife Ani, thank you for filling my world with love.

Introduction

Can We Take Hold Of Our History?

The Texas State Capitol was built in its own very Texan way. After the Civil War, it was designed to stand fifteen feet taller than its counterpart in Washington. But, short on cash, the state government traded around 3 million acres of public land to a group of out-of-state investors to build it. To keep costs down, the state government also leased some 500 convict laborers for the project. Naturally, this pissed off the local unions, who had been asked to oversee the building's construction. They refused to help with the project, at which point the Syndicate turned to foreign scab labor as a substitute. 86 Scotsmen out of Aberdeen descended on Austin to help complete the project. When the Scots discovered they were scabs, 24 refused to work. Ultimately, the Capitol was built, and the Syndicate successfully argued a court-mandated fine for violating labor laws down from $64,000 to $8,000, which the International Association of Granite Cutters angrily argued was clearly the result of the backroom deals.[1] If you grew up here, as I did, this story sounds all too familiar.

Like the Alamo or the towering monument to the Battle of San Jacinto, where Mexican General Santa Anna surrendered to Sam Houston, the Capitol remains a symbol of Texan-ness, a visceral connection to our history, though usually the mythic version. Most Texans don't know about the labor struggle that birthed the Texas Capitol. But upon learning the story, it doesn't exactly flip the world on its axis. When people ask why Texas is the way it is—a bastion of conservatism—people can point to the Capitol and say, "Labor loses in Texas." The story goes that Texans prefer conservatism, so-called states' rights, and personal independence. But this wasn't a foregone conclusion. It required the full force of the state to defeat many generations of Texas radicals, in labor and in politics. Even today, from time to time, you might catch a glimpse of a different kind of Texas. You might hear it in the chants of workers on strike, or in the clamor of mass protests. You might see it in the eyes of canvassers marching from house to house to tell you about their candidate. Perhaps you've felt it too, but often as soon as you have, it's gone again. Snuffed out. Why?

Back in 2018, everyone was abuzz with possibility: Could Texas actually go blue? The hype began early that March, when Beto O'Rourke—a skateboard-loving El Paso Congressman with a penchant for standing and speaking on tabletops—handily won the Democratic primary. He'd already won the hearts and minds of national media, but his scrappy, social media-savvy campaign soon won the support of a lot of average Texans who were tired of the likes of his opponent, the Canadian-born Tea Party Republican Ted Cruz. In Austin, the city was littered with Beto O'Rourke yard signs. Even today, nearly a decade later, it's not uncommon to see his signature "Whataburger" inspired bumper stickers on cars of all kinds. Having lived through a few of these hype cycles that Texas might finally "turn blue," I had my doubts, but Beto's campaign did something exciting. They were willing to travel and hold rallies all across the state. This kind of confidence—not just a belief that Texas is winnable, but a belief that Texans who had gone to the Republican Party could be won over—was something different from a Texas Democrat. Beto wasn't hiding in the state's safe blue areas; he was challenging the narrative of what Texas is, and what it could be.

It was not to be. On election night, Ted Cruz won again, by just over 2 percentage points. In its appraisal of the Beto campaign, the *Texas Observer* found that the results were a reminder that "Texas is still more like the state that has unflinchingly elected Trump, Ted Cruz, Greg Abbott, Dan Patrick, Rick Perry, and George W. Bush" than the one Beto tried to win.[2] Beto appeared to many destined for some sort of higher office, but he failed to replicate the enthusiasm in his 2020 bid for president. More embarrassingly, in his 2022 campaign for governor, he lost to Abbott by nearly 11 points. Folks had been briefly willing to question the common wisdom that Texans will always be Republicans, but the dream was shattered yet again. In subsequent races, fewer were willing to suspend their disbelief.

Those who believed that Beto had run "too liberal" and that Texas Democrats would fare better with a more conservative Democrat got their chance in 2024. Colin Allred's failed Senate campaign was in many ways the polar opposite of Beto's 2018 run. Allred swapped big rallies for small gatherings, unscripted moments for television ads, and reminder after reminder that he played in the NFL. Where Beto had called out Trump's border wall as "a racist reaction to a racist myth,"[3] Allred voted with Republicans in the House of Representatives to "condemn

Biden's Open Border policies." Even in defeat, the two typified very different approaches to politics: In 2018, Beto took to the stage and told a cheering crowd, "I am so fucking proud of you guys," whereas Allred, ever reserved, quoted the conservative prime minister Winston Churchill—"you can't just be a patriot when your side wins."[4] Meanwhile, in the six years separating their candidacies, the voter margin slipped further in Republicans' favor.

* * *

Clearly, something isn't working. Beto's campaign aimed to make good on the old Democratic maxim that "Texas isn't a red state, it's a non-voting state," by campaigning across the state's 254 counties—from blue Travis County, where Austin resides, to red Borden County, which went over 90 percent to Trump in 2024. He had a bold ground game, mixed with what sounded like unabashed progressivism, though the details were often murky. In any case, this was a bottom-up operation, from its field offices to its voter database, driven by a passionate team of volunteers. By contrast, Allred only visited 34 of Texas's 254 counties while raising a historic $90.2 million, much of which came from out of state,[5] and heavily relied on TV ads in Texas's 20 media markets. Needless to say, the two campaigns had different target audiences in mind.

Here's another Democratic maxim you may have heard: "Demographics as destiny." On one hand, Texas's growing Hispanic population, which has overtaken Anglos as the largest ethnic group in the state, drove the belief that victory for the Democratic Party would mean channeling greater Hispanic electoral participation. (Hence Beto's Spanish flourishes on the debate stage.) On the other hand, Democrats looked to the growing liberalization of the suburbs—Republican strongholds, once upon a time, which have shifted blue in recent years as the more educated and affluent class slouches toward the center-left. (Hence Allred's lackluster strategy.) Lastly, as Texas's population surged, Democrats believed this would bring friendlier voters into the fold, pushing their margins over the top. While Beto's may have been a more active and excited campaign, and Allred's a more passive reaping, both were driven by the idea that one needn't change voters' minds so much as collect the greatest naturally occurring assortment of votes. This belief that *voters* must change, not politics, is key to understanding Democrats' strategy over the past decade. If the demographics were right enough, the thinking went, Democrats would win. But look a little deeper and you'll find a much more interesting picture.

For instance, in 2018, Ted Cruz held onto his seat not because he appealed to some deep-rooted Texan tradition—but because he overwhelmingly won among voters who had moved to Texas. Had the race been limited to only native Texans—that is, people born in the state—Beto O'Rourke would have *won* the native-Texan vote fifty-one percent to forty-eight percent.[6] It was the new Texans who put Ted Cruz over the top. While Republicans ironically bandy the "Don't California My Texas!" slogan across the campaign trail—claiming in so many words that outsiders are spoiling Texas politics—these new Texans aren't turning Texas blue. They're disproportionately voting Republican, no matter how much Democrats may wish they weren't.[7]

Indeed, internal migration has been key to GOP success in Texas for decades. In the 1970s and 1980s, the Republican Party was boosted to competitiveness in large part due to GOP voters from out of state who moved to the Texas cities and suburbs—part of a broader population shift within what's called the Sun Belt, which runs across the Southern United States from Florida to California. This change was something a then-young Republican strategist, Karl Rove, understood well. He helped the party achieve its complete takeover of the state by capitalizing on the demographic changes in Texas in the 1980s, notably the migration of Republican voters from the Midwest to the Texas suburbs. While Rove correctly saw the favorable demographic changes, the Texas GOP, unlike Democrats, did more than catch a favorable wind in their sails. The GOP built a sizable and influential organization, encouraging grassroots supporters, women, and young people inspired by Ronald Reagan to do much of the party's on-the-ground work.

A Democrat has not won statewide office in Texas since 1994, and they haven't had enough seats to control the State House or Senate for more than two decades. One might expect this to have translated into political stability. It hasn't. The lack of a threat from the Democratic Party has allowed the Republicans to wage a bitter civil war. Some of these fights have been over policy, like the now-passed school voucher program. For years, rural Republicans opposed school vouchers, as schools tend to be not only a major employer in rural Texas but also a cultural center for the community. That was before Texas oil billionaire Tim Dunn, with the help of a few billionaire friends, fired a money cannon at Republican incumbents seen as opposed to their agenda. Dunn and his PAC backed twenty-eight challengers to established Republicans, and won fifteen of those races. A school voucher system was passed in the 2025 legislative session by a vote of 86 to 63. The conflict is not always so material; sometimes it's about loyalty. Entire NGO and media operations are dedicated to waging this war inside the GOP. One of the more prevalent ones is the Texas Scorecard, which publishes documentaries such as "Red Power," which opens asking if China "could take down our power grid" with wind power, or another claiming the Texas legislature is controlled by Democrats pretending to be Republicans. When Dustin Burrows won the speakers' race, right-wing activists pondered the big questions: could the Lubbock Republican be a Democrat plant?

Despite all the infighting, Democrats have not been able to take advantage. Since Rove, Texas's population has not stopped booming.[8] Between 1970 and 2022, its population grew by 166 percent, from around 11 million people to a whopping 30 million. (During the same period, the U.S. population only grew by roughly 63 percent.) Despite our rural reputation, Texas is second only to California in its share of urban population in the country, and 83.7% of Texans live in urban areas.[9] And in Texas's major cities, Democrats are dominant, with centrists, liberals, progressives, and even democratic socialists competing for power in a manner similar to New York or California. Members of the Democratic Socialists of America have won seats on the San Antonio and Austin city councils. National figures like Congressman Greg Casar, leader of the progressive caucus, first won election in Austin with the help of a coalition including organized labor, DSA, and other progressive NGOs.

Across the state, ballot initiatives have been used to win goals like bail reform and marijuana decriminalization. But rather than build upon these local gains at the state level, campaigns like Allred's adhere to the idea that the only way to win over rural areas is by tacking rightward.

This "realist" strategy's track record has been unimpressive. To be fair, there are plenty of conservatives in Texas, and there were before this long wave of internal migration. In Allred's case, his signaling to the right did not win him converts, nor did it prevent Ted Cruz from portraying him as an out-of-touch coastal-elite liberal.

Why is this political anxiety about California so effective for Republican politicians? First and foremost, it paints their party in a good light: To be Texan is to be a conservative Republican, so by being a Republican, you get to be a "real Texan" too. Those *other* political persuasions are propped up by carpet-bagging elitists; they could never understand what makes our beloved state great. But more importantly, the anxiety people feel is real—Texas is changing for the worse. While the state continues to boom economically, working-class people are being squeezed. By blaming all of these changes on California—what I'll call the California Hypothesis—politicians use our new neighbors as an excuse for the consequences of their own actions, selling us out to the billionaire class.

For much of the 20th century, the Texas economy was defined by the boom and bust cycle of oil. But following the 1980s, the Texas economy diversified and its economy soared. A lot of this has been driven by corporate relocation, a trend that continues today. Meanwhile, for a state where the world's wealthiest man resides, poverty in Texas is astonishingly high, and it's not just due to its geographic size. High poverty is as much an urban as it is a rural crisis, from Houston, the fourth-largest metropolitan area in the U.S., which leads the nation's major cities in poverty and has a childhood poverty rate at an astonishing 20.3%,[10] to rural and long underserved South Texas, which swung hard for Trump in 2024, where childhood poverty is as high as 33%.[11] Nor is this due to a lack of hard work. Texas regularly ranks among the top in the nation for time spent at work, but that hasn't made Texans wealthier. Texans' median household income trails that of California by over $20,000 a year, and Texas's $79,721 median household income sits under the national average.[12] Texans work more and make less. But despite the poverty amongst working-class Texans, there is plenty of money being made. While Texan governors like Greg Abbott and Rick Perry may tout the so-called "Texas miracle"—that our home state is the eighth-largest economy in the world—the reality for working-class Texans is that times are only getting tougher.

The fact is, taking Texas's low wages into account, that Texas workers are being exploited to fuel the profits for the idle rich. For decades, the Texas GOP has led an onslaught against unions while providing special protections for big business, building up a tax system that punishes the poor to subsidize corporate handouts. While working-class Texans fueled this economic boom, it was the idle classes, the bankers, the CEOs, and the stockholders who benefited. Over a hundred years ago now, Texas cotton farmers gathered together to ask themselves a similar question. Why was it that those "who work most get least, and those who work least get most?"[13] These questions are just as critical today as they were at the birth of Texan populism, and if we are to take on these same forces again, understanding what worked and what didn't in the past will be necessary.

***

You'll get no reflection on the consequences of three decades of GOP rule if Texas Republicans can redirect that anxiety into their favorite pastime, waging culture war. Why would they? Take something like our open carry gun laws. A UT/Texas Tribune poll found that fifty-nine percent of Texans oppose it.[14] So-called "Constitutional carry" is not only unpopular, it's out of step with Texas history. In 1871, Texas passed sweeping limitations on open and concealed carry—not just of pistols and handguns, but daggers, and even bowie knives.[15] For the vast majority of Texas history, the open carry rules of today are far outside of the norm.

Republicans in Texas have been skillful at crafting a version of Texas history that is favorable to their current goals. And they are not afraid of using their political power to enforce this narrative. In recent years, the Texas Legislature has turned its eye toward high school and higher education curricula, enforcing a more conservative view of U.S. and Texas history. At the Alamo, Lt. Governor Dan Patrick led a personal crusade to fire Alamo Trust Inc. President and CEO Kate Rogers, who manages the site, over her views on teaching about the indigenous history of the region, as well as her hope that the Alamo can serve as "a beacon for historical reconciliation and a place that brings people together versus tearing them apart."[16] The fact that maintaining a particular politicized view of Texas history requires very active enforcement from conservative politicians shows that it's not some natural outgrowth of simple facts. It's a concerted effort for Texas to be seen in a certain light.

But Texas has a rich history of liberalism, which has made it difficult for the GOP to remake the state in its own image completely. For most of its history, the Democratic Party dominated politics, and while business-friendly conservatives were abundant, there was plenty of room for more New Deal-friendly politicians like Lyndon B. Johnson. You can still see the effects of this history today. It took tremendous sums of money and political pressure for Greg Abbott and other conservative politicians to force rural Republicans, of all people, to support their school voucher program, initiating the potential destruction of the public school system as we know it. That's because New Deal liberalism, however divorced from its own history, remains popular with Texans. Other figures, such as Barbara Jordan, elected to Congress in 1972, represent a connected, yet distinct, version of Texas liberalism; much can be learned from studying her pragmatic yet unapologetic fight for civil rights in Texas and beyond.

Texas also has a deep tradition of political radicalism. Many will be surprised to learn that Texas once was home to one of the largest Socialist Party chapters in the United States. The party, which reached its height in the early 1910s, advocated many demands that will seem familiar today: Universal healthcare, protections for workers, taxing the super-rich, and taking industries under public control. But they were also explicit that without a direct confrontation with capital, their dream of a "cooperative commonwealth" would never be realized. Before that, cowboys once banded together to take on the unchecked power of the cattle barons: The cowboy, a symbol of rugged individualism often used as a stand-in for conservatism, was a lot more collectively minded than the John Wayne-style caricatures allow. Indeed, Populism, the precursor to American Socialism, whose legacy held a significant influence on what would become the New Deal, was born here, in Texas.

How we view ourselves matters. The story that Texas, or America for that matter, is inherently conservative is regularly employed to stifle progressive policies and justify running right-leaning Democrats instead of candidates who will fight for the working class. The problem is that this assumption is based on a false understanding of Texans and Texas history. And as Colin Allred's disastrous campaign showed, tailing the Republican Party doesn't work. Instead, we should draw on Texas's under-appreciated history of working-class politics—unapologetic in its rejection of rule by economic elites, and self-assured in its belief that a better world is possible.

Reconnecting with the deep-rooted tradition of Texas radicals will give our movement the confidence to boldly advocate for our values and provide us with the hard-won lessons of our heritage. While stories of poor cotton farmers and landless cowboys may feel far off from today, there is much that connects us. Questions of identity as the state population booms today are not so far off from the shifts of the 19th century. Like the tenant farmers of the last century, workers today do not own their own workplaces or tools, and live at the mercy of their bosses.

Even modern gig work arrangements like Uber driving, where a worker may own their car, are predicated on debt, much like the crop-lien system that tormented Texans a century ago. If we want to beat the Right in Texas, let alone everywhere else, we must, as the historian Harvey Kaye urges, "take hold of our history."

This book is a modest attempt to do so. I will not tell the entire history of Texas, or give an exhaustive history of the Texan left; instead, this book introduces radical moments in Texas's history with important lessons for the left today. "Radical" is often treated like a dirty word, something extreme and out of touch. But it has a long history in the U.S. to describe politics that seek to meet the needs of everyday people, in a system that often feels designed to exploit them and their labor. As the New Deal was coming into being, Franklin Delano Roosevelt, a president who profoundly shaped our political culture, used the word in a positive light, saying, "It is time for the country to become fairly radical for a generation."[17] The movements described in this book sought to go much further than the New Deal. They were "radical" in the sense that they were challenging the governing ideals of the country, but those ideals had become unacceptable to the masses.

In Part 1, we will survey Texas Populism, a movement of farmers who dared to challenge the "money power" in Texas, and nearly toppled the "party of their fathers," the Democratic Party, backed by the land barons and the rich, which had dominated southern politics for generations. In Part 2, we'll see the rise and fall of the Texas Socialist Party, which, despite unfavorable conditions, continued the farmers' revolt, connecting it with labor struggles and the Mexican Revolution to put fear in the ruling class of Texas. In Part 3, we'll look at the New Deal Era and the labor fights that engulfed San Antonio, where Mexican American and Tejano workers demanded that they live in dignity.

This is not a revisionist history. Texas history is filled with plenty of horrors. This work seeks to present the other side, showcasing those who, in their own way, fought for justice against powerful interests. They often came up short. But through the decades, they crafted a unique Texas tradition of opposition to those in power, which may point to how we might build a better world today.

Texas farmers in the Gilded Age feared they would be worse off than their parents. Many were correct to think so. While robber barons fattened themselves on government handouts, debt had forced farmers into tenancy, with some even becoming renters on the land their family once owned. But these farmers joined in large collective organizations and united with organized labor to demand that the government act in the people's interests—not just the rich.

The Knights of Labor and the Brotherhood of Timber Workers, some of the nation's first labor organizations with a strong presence in Texas, would have to fight for the right to organize. With no roadmap, these trailblazing labor leaders cut their own path through a hostile environment and fought against an enmeshed alliance between their bosses and Texas politicians. Today, union density is historically low, and the working class is not organized politically. Like the early Texas Populists, Socialists, and labor unions, the hard work we must do is ahead of us. But learning lessons from the past will help guide us. The questions these people asked are similar to those we face today. How best to build a working-class political movement? Should we reform the Democratic Party, build a third-party movement, or stay out of electoral politics entirely? How do we organize under increasing state surveillance and even repression? How do we cultivate leaders from the grassroots, engage in political education, and build independent media to challenge corporate control of the press? How do we connect the fight for economic, racial, and social justice together, all at once? And importantly, how do we build a community that can withstand setbacks—and equally important, how do we build one capable of celebrating victories? All of these questions, hotly debated today, were equally important to the Texas radicals.

This story is not so much about why we do not have a strong left or a labor movement today. It is the story of how those movements were crushed by corporate power and the government, and how these radical roots were buried and became forgotten. But like the bluebonnets, which can lie dormant for years waiting for favorable conditions to grow, the Texas radical tradition can—and must—blossom again. Our state is changing; the American Dream is out of reach for many, and our democracy is in crisis, unresponsive to the needs and wants of the people. Can we take inspiration from those who came before, from those who fought for a better life for themselves and those around them? What if we looked not to the Texas Capitol as a beacon of what it means to be Texan, but to the many workers who built it instead?

PART I

The Birth of Populism

Chapter 1

A Dying Frontier

In the late 1870s, if you were thinking about starting a new life out West, a Panhandle town like Tascosa, Texas, nestled on the banks of the Canadian River, around thirty miles from Amarillo, might've seemed like a good bet. With a booming cattle trail to Dodge City, Kansas, cutting through Tascosa, the town was drawing the attention of all kinds of troublemakers, from outlaws like Billy the Kid to Northern businessmen set on getting their hands on the land, the cattle, and most importantly, the profits that came with them.

Before the area was called Tascosa, it was a holdout for an alliance of Comanche, Southern Cheyenne, Arapaho, and Kiowa warriors who sought to live outside the reservations in Oklahoma created by the U.S. government. In 1874, the alliance gathered thousands of pounds of buffalo meat and supplies and found shelter from the cruel Panhandle winter in Palo Duro Canyon, which had long served as a refuge to the area's first peoples. However, a group of Tonkawa scouts found the settlement and alerted the U.S. Army of their location. Colonel Ronald S. Mackenzie soon led a raid on the camp, in what was later named the Battle of Palo Duro. Caught by surprise, the warriors, under the leadership of a Kiowa Chief Lone Wolf, had no choice but to retreat. Though the battle led to few casualties—save for the nearly 1,500 horses that Mackenzie had ordered his men to shoot—the Comanche, Southern Cheyenne, Arapaho, and Kiowa, with no chance to survive without the torched supplies and horses, were forced to return to the reservations in Oklahoma on foot.

Two years later, a sheep rancher, Casimero Romero, settled the land that would become Tascosa. Romero bet that the trail up to Dodge City would make the area a hotspot for local trade. Then misfortune hit: A cold winter killed half of his flock. He took up work in Dodge City for a few years before returning to Tascosa. But, in his absence, the sheep town he had settled was now a booming cattle town, with a saloon and a hotel to boot. Romero's dreams were among the first of many casualties in the war between the Big Men, backed with money and political connections, and the Little Men, who worked with their hands to make their way in life. As land became scarce across Texas and the West, every man would need to pick a side.

The cattle drives, which were made famous in movies and novels like *Lonesome Dove,* came out of economic necessity. Texas had not seen much conflict in the Civil War, but the state was economically devastated. There was a need for a major export to bring dollars into Texas, and the state's answer was beef. In Texas, where cattle were plentiful, beef wouldn't fetch much of a price. But if you could get your cattle up to a major market—particularly those on the East Coast—they'd pay ten times per head what they were worth in San Antonio. As spring approached, ranchers and their hands would "round up" their cattle, hiring extra workers, to prepare for long drives to reach the railroads in Missouri or Kansas. It was tough, boring, and dangerous work. But with money to be made, all sorts tried their luck, especially the young.

By the 1880s, Tascosa was booming. Successful cattle drives brought with them plenty of money, plenty of workers, and plenty of investment opportunities. Cattle drives had at first been an almost laughably absurd scheme by a few desperate Texans with little choice but to find a decent market for their cattle. But when those upstarts proved this crazy idea was not only possible but profitable, capitalists took notice.

Like the beef-rich Texans who found voracious buyers in the beef-starved North, Northern and European capitalists discovered their money went far in cash-starved Texas. While the U.S. Army violently cleared the land of its Native peoples in the Indian Wars, the poverty in Texas provided a perfect opportunity for large land grabs. It didn't take long for far-off owners to gobble up large tracts of land in and around Tascosa (and across the Lone Star State). For these soon-to-be land barons, understanding the law—especially creative interpretations of the law—was more important than knowing how to run a ranch.

So-called "lease laws" in Texas were easy for land grabbers to exploit: "if a lessee had built as much as one hundred dollars' worth of improvement," he had a claim on the land "without danger of being bought out or having the land leased by someone else."[1] Puzzled small landowners found minor improvements on their land and out on the open range, built by the deep-pocketed large ranchers. These "improvements," far from a neighborly gift, were used to dispossess small landowners or "nesters" in court. Many of these "small-folk" schooled in the old ways could not or did not know how to produce the documentation needed to protect their claims; sometimes, there hadn't even been a lease on the land in the first place. The fact that many of the judges and lawmen in town were friendly with—and, in some cases, employed by—the big ranchers dissuaded the rightfully angry small people from making too public a fuss.

Money and legal tricks can get you land, but to work it, you need people. As the names and brands of ranches changed, so did cowboy work in Texas. In Tascosa, the new landowners wanted to get more with less: to "modernize" the work, turning the centuries-old vaquero traditions into common wage labor. The storied cowboy was becoming what E.M. Rhodes called the "hired man on horseback." Notable among the changes was the banning of cowboys from mavericking. Cattle were plentiful in Texas, and cowboys frequently came across unowned cattle called "mavericks" while working their herds. Tradition dictated that working cowboys could claim at least a portion of these, and that they could graze alongside the employer's larger herd. This was more than a little bonus; it was their chance to start their own herd and climb the ladder. However, the new landowners cared little for the Old West's traditions, and these laborers raising their own cattle smelled like competition. The new bosses demanded the cowboys work only for a wage. The old Texas was dying, the logic of the frontier replaced by the logic of the ledger. Soon, the open range would be squeezed by jagged and bloodied barbed wire.

Chapter 2

Cowboys on Strike

In 1883, three wagon bosses—Thomas B. Harris, Roy Griffin, and J.W. Peacock—got together to discuss the threats to their line of work. As wagon bosses, these men oversaw their fellow cowboys and regularly interacted with the ranch bosses. They were also highly paid, but they were not paid off. With the industry becoming ever more punishing to the average cowboy, and the spring cattle drive to Dodge City nearly underway, these wagon bosses understood something needed to be done. They decided to organize a meet-up of all concerned cowpunchers around Tascosa.

At the meet-up, cowhands quickly understood these changes brought on by the ranch bosses would mean they could never get ahead. Cowboying was a young man's game, and without mavericking, low-wage work would mean their end. So instead of competing amongst each other, they created an association and promised to bargain for wages together, across all of the significant cattle ranches in the region. The men signed the following statement:

> We, the undersigned cowboys of Canadian River, do by these presents agree to bind ourselves into the following obligations, viz—First, that we will not work for less than $50 per

month, and we furthermore agree no one shall work for less than $50 per month, after 31st of March.

Second, good cooks shall also receive $50 per month. Third, anyone running an outfit shall not work for less than $75 per month. Anyone violating the above obligations shall suffer the consequences. Those not having funds to pay board after March 31st will be provided for 30 days at Tascosa.

Signed Thomas Harris, Roy Griffin, J. W. Peacock, J. L. Howard, W. S. Gaton, S. G. Brown, W. B. Borina, D. W. Peeples, James Jones, C. M. Hullett, V. F. Martin, Harry Ingerton, J. S. Morris, Jim Miller, Henry Stafford, William F. Kerr, Bull Davis, T. D. Holliday, C. F. Goddard, E. E. Watkins, C. B. Thompson, G. F. Nickell, Juan A. Gomez, and J. L. Grisson.[2]

For a regular cowpuncher, $50 was a significant pay raise from the $20 or so a month they had previously earned, and $75 per month was a marked improvement for wagon bosses. Thomas Harris and the others organized a strike fund to ensure cowboys were fed and taken care of while on strike, and the cowboys made their camp near "west of Mitchell Canyon."[3] With their intentions set to paper, and the timing just right—early spring, when the price per head was best—the cowboys went on strike.

While many accounts contend that the strike began on March 31, 1883, it more likely started as early as March 23. In historian Mark Lause's excellent account, the conflicting starting dates were likely caused by differing start dates for each respective cattle drive.[4] Most workers weren't scheduled to start work until March 31, so the walkouts beginning on March 23 were smaller. What isn't debated is the severe reaction from the ranchers. A late arrival in Dodge City meant significant losses in the cattle trade. When wagon boss J.W. Peacock rode out with the negotiating team to meet with representatives from the LIT Ranch, he was offered a half-measure raise. Peacock and the others refused to sell out the striking workers so cheaply. So the LIT representative reminded them of their place, reclaiming the horses that the striking cowboys had ridden out on as company property. Peacock and his comrades were forced to walk back to camp over many miles.[5]

While the battered and windswept lands may be a different backdrop from the industrial setting of most labor disputes, the tactics were similar. One of the owners of the LS Ranch was a man named W.M.D. Lee. Born in Pennsylvania, he made his money in the brutal buffalo hunts that nearly eradicated the species.[6] When the strike began, W.M.D. Lee was up in Dodge City. He rushed back down to Texas and lambasted his enforcer, McAllister, for the work stoppage. Lee allegedly told McAllister that he should have agreed to the cowboys in word and hired scabs at a lower wage as soon as he got the chance.[7]

Having missed this opportunity, W.M.D. Lee tried again to break the solidarity of this cowpuncher union. He called the wagon boss and strike leader, Thomas Harris, to his house for a one-on-one conversation. Harris was already making $100 a month, double what regular cowboys were asking for. W.M.D. Lee, knowing nothing of solidarity, could not understand why Harris was sticking his neck out for these "nester boys," and offered a compromise: if Harris would call off the strike, he would pay $50 a month for a small group of "top hands" chosen by Harris, and he would keep Harris in his employ.[8] The bribery failed. Thomas Harris refused and rode out to camp with his fellow striking workers, proving himself to his men and the labor movement.

The sides were set. The striking cowboys hung around camp and in Tascosa, spreading the word of the strike and discouraging would-be scabs from working at the big ranches. That cowboys in the 1880s were armed should surprise no one, and while it makes for a good tale, there were no credible incidents of violence. This did not stop newspapermen all over the country from printing the most salacious stories they heard—stories of anarchy and drunkenness in equal measure. This was largely because employers had an "unchecked monopoly on documenting the strike," as Mark Lause argues.[9] The employers "regularly sent their representatives to visit the rail heads and larger cities,"[10] where reporters were happy to print whatever the bosses' mouthpieces told them. Much like today, the bosses of the time understood that information warfare was a powerful tool. For example, the *Las Vegas Gazette* warned of an imminent march of the Texas State militia on the Panhandle ordered by Texas Governor Oran M. Roberts to put down the "rebellion." This did not happen. Not only was there no mobilization of the state militia, Roberts wasn't even the governor anymore, having been replaced by Governor John Ireland in January 1883.[11]

The wildly inaccurate news stories of the time have led to speculation about the results of the Great Cowboy Strike of 1883.

One of the most popular accounts, written by historian Robert E. Zeigler, first published in 1952 and still treated as the final authority on the matter, claims that the cowboys lost. He ends by calling the strike an "interesting but isolated incident that had no lasting repercussions for either cowboys or the cattle industry."[12] Zeigler rightfully agrees that "no violence occurred," but he seems to take the big ranchers at their word, accepting without question that they "fired striking employees … continued with roundup plans by hiring replacement workers at temporarily increased wages" and "after 2 ½ months the strike was so weakened that the may roundup occurred without incident."[13]

Zeigler's article on the Cowboy Strike, first published in 1952, is repeated by many contemporary accounts—a testament to how certain historical narratives become cemented as fact through repetition. For instance, a *Texas Co-op Power* article on the topic ends by quoting Zeigler's characterization that the strike was "an interesting but isolated incident."[14] Even the Texas AFL-CIO, while acknowledging the importance of this event, repeats the story told by the ranch bosses relayed by Zeigler that the undisciplined cowboys dried up their strike fund "drinking and gambling in Tascosa."[15]

What if the tale of rowdy and individualistic cowpunchers unable to organize was wrong? What if instead of an "interesting and isolated event" ending in failure, the cowboy strike was another chapter in a deep and overlooked history of everyday Texans organizing and banding together against a powerful capitalist class? If the big ranchers were willing to lie about the conduct of the striking cowboys while the strike was on, would it not stand to reason that they might lie about the results of the strike itself? In fact, the U.S. Commissioner of Labor reported at the time that the Cowboy Strike was a success. The dry account records a victory for striking workers in the Texas Panhandle and notes a forty-two percent increase in daily wages for the cowboys "from $1.18 to $1.68."[16] Not only did the U.S. government report note the victories for the striking workers; it also noted the big ranches suffered, a "collective loss of $3,835."[17]

As Mark Lause argues, the strike in early spring, the height of cattle drive season, "was so well planned, well timed, and well executed that it won a quick victory," having forced the ranch owners to accept their demands or lose valuable profits.[18] Thomas B. Harris, Roy Griffin, J.W. Peacock, and around three hundred other cowboys took on these new bosses of the West and won. The belief that working people banding together to take on the power of concentrated wealth wasn't the result of some foreign agitation or romantic dream of idealists. It was a homegrown, practical response to the abuses of a creeping form of capitalism that would forever change the state of Texas.

It was a meaningful victory, but not without consequences. Afterwards, most of the strike leaders were blacklisted, unable to work. The LS boss W.M.D. Lee carried around a thorough list of names of everyone involved in the strike.[19] Thomas Harris headed west into New Mexico and worked to form a cooperative ranching venture with some of his fellow strikers that went by many names, including "The Get Even Cattle Company."[20] Their operation was a source of fury for their former bosses and accusations of foul play proliferated. The established ranchers complained that their cattle was being stolen and rebranded by these upstarts. It's not unlikely that some folks were, in fact, altering the brands on the major ranches' cattle. In recent years, with the practice of mavericking slowly becoming prohibited, even marking an unmarked cow could be construed as rustling. But what some called rustling, others might've called taking what's rightfully theirs. Philosophical questions aside, ranch owners had a tough time proving mass cattle rustling. In Tascosa, the Oldham County Commissioners Court attempted to adjudicate these claims but ultimately failed.

Despite all of the bias in favor of the cattle barons, it was the small cowboys who, in fact, won a legal victory against the cattle barons. Deputized men from the LS and LIT Ranches butchered thirty-five heads of cattle that belonged to Bill Gatlin, who rode with strike leader Thomas Harris,[21] and quickly sold the meat. But they were eventually forced to pay $25,000 in damages.[22] It was a rare victory. Soon, the Texas government chose a side—the side of the rich.

The now-mythic story of Pat Garrett shooting the outlaw Billy the Kid, in New Mexico in 1881, often serves as a curtain call for the Old West. Like the Cowboy Strike, interpretations abound. Did Billy the Kid die quickly, or did he lay in agony for days before passing? The answer is lost to history. But one certainty remains: Law and order was coming, paying special heed to the interests of the rich and the white, delivered by state-sanctioned vigilantes in a crude, callous, and, in this case, cowardly way—to shots fired at an unarmed man by a Sheriff hiding behind a curtain.

And who would the cattle barons call but Pat Garrett to rid the land of these class-conscious cowboys. The cattle barons claimed they had gotten permission from Governor John Ireland to organize "home rangers" to deal with the alleged rustlers.[23] There exists no record of this order, so the governor must have given direction to Pat Garrett himself either orally or in a private letter.[24] This special appeal was granted despite the cattle barons' failure to prove their losses in a court of law. In practice, these men were little more than deputized armed guards of the LS Ranch, where they lodged, took their meals, and even worked the cattle on the ranch. They were known by most not as home rangers but as "LS Rangers," in honor of who they truly represented—the bosses.

The final chapter of the great cowboy strikers ended in a tense but bloodless showdown between Pat Garrett and his deputized posse and the former strike leaders. Garrett and his men got 159 indictments to chase down the men, most accused of "stock theft." Additionally, the cattle barons convinced Governor Ireland to declare an ordinance against "carrying six-shooters."[25] The ban, as absurd as outlawing the wearing of cowboy hats, had nothing to do with public safety, but it gave Pat Garrett and his "LS Rangers" justification to harass whomever they pleased. Neither were the indictments designed to hold up in court, but to aid Garrett and his men in their real mission: Ridding the area of the strikers.[26]

In February 1885, Garrett heard that Harris and other members of the cooperative were at a stone house off the Canadian River. Garrett waited for a storm to ensure it'd be hard for Harris and his friends to escape, and rode out. Arriving at the snowed-in cabin, Pat Garrett surrounded the house and requested three men—known members of the cooperative, Bill Gatlin, Charlie Thompson, and Wade Woods—to surrender themselves. Thomas Harris stepped out; once again, he'd represent working cowboys against representatives of the LS Ranch.

Despite the popular narratives about the cowboy strikers, Harris and his company were quite civilized. Harris told the LS Rangers they had no desire for a shootout. Wade Woods wasn't in the cabin, but Charlie Thompson surrendered himself. Gatlin took some convincing; he was initially unwilling to hand himself over to the killer of Billy the Kid, now a deputized enforcer for the cattle barons who no doubt would have enjoyed seeing Gatlin hanged. Eventually, Garrett entered the house alone to reason with Gatlin, who allowed himself to be taken to avoid a shootout. Privately, Garrett began to doubt his presence in Tascosa had anything to do with law and order.[27] When the last man exited the cabin, Garrett sent his compatriots to disassemble the house.[28]

The town lacked a jailhouse, so the prisoners were chained up inside an abandoned building. But while the government had taken the side of the cattle barons, the people hadn't. Late in the night, with the aid of the townspeople, the men escaped their confinement.[29] They made their escape, but the message was clear: the bosses owned the land, the government, and the law. With the aid of the state government and known killers, the area would not be safe much longer for those willing to challenge the tightening rule of the money power.

* * *

The cowboy strike was not an "isolated incident." The strikers may have lost their jobs, but they set a new standard for higher wages for cowboys in the region and across the industry. Along with government data proving this wage victory, even sympathetic histories of the LS Ranch bragged that following the strike all wagon bosses "drew seventy-five dollars a month."[30] Beyond the effect on the Panhandle, this conflict is an important moment in Texas history. Over the next few decades, as Texas workers began to organize themselves into unions, they were accused of being egged on by outside forces and ideas. Labor conflict was treated as something foreign, imported into Texas by outside agitators. This was nonsense then just as it is today. Solidarity, and fighting for what you were due, were present from the very beginning of Texas's shift from the frontier to the industrial and agrarian empire it would soon become.

So why, then, is the historical record of the 1883 Cowboy Strike so muddied? The history of these Texas cowboys—workers with shared interests—runs against the Hollywood trope of cowboys as the embodiment of individualism: "It is the value system of the rugged individual we call the cowboy that explains the lack of the class struggle," wrote the historian William H. Hutchinson, in his 1972 essay, "The Cowboy and the Class Struggle (Or, Never Put Marx in the Saddle)."[31] This view of history gorges itself on every cliche imaginable, arguing that the cowboy, "never could see the class struggle's vision of him and his fellows as helpless victims in life's abattoir."[32] Dress up your argument however you like. The simple fact is that when Thomas Harris turned down his boss's offer to break the strike and preserve his $100-a-month position, it was not because of a "value system of the rugged individual." Call it neighborliness, bravery, or simply looking out for the men riding next to you on that day in Old Tascosa. In any case, being a cowboy in those days—not just working on the range, but more broadly, living by Texan values—meant solidarity.

Chapter 3

The Coming of Barbed Wire

In 1885, two years after the Great Cowboy Strike, blizzards swept from the north across the Texas Panhandle. Unlike the buffalo, who turn to face the bad weather, when cattle smell a storm like this one, they (quite reasonably) move in the opposite direction. Picture these massive herds shuffling southward, toward safety and warmth of the canyons and valleys they traditionally sought in bad weather. Unbeknownst to them, they were marching to their death.

The once open-range grasslands were now covered with miles upon miles of so-called "drift fences," consisting largely of barbed wire, which landowners used to stake their claim on broad swaths of territory. As a result, these herds pushed up against the fences but were unable to pass. They walked the seemingly never-ending fence line as the freezing winds cut through them. Eventually, the panicked cattle pressed against each other for warmth, a final respite as the cold closed in. When the storms receded, cowboys found mountains of frozen cattle huddled upon one another. One cowboy in the Texas Panhandle described the scene:

"I could have walked for miles on dead animals, stepping from one to another. These were mostly natives belonging to northern ranges which had drifted across the burned prairie. As long as they could travel, cattle kept alive. Finally, the drift fence halted them. Here they stopped … bunched close together as for a last protection, helplessly dropped in their tracks and froze."[33]

This was the great "Die-Up" of 1885-86. The land in Texas and across the West was changing. The previous decade had seen abundant rain, which nourished the grasslands of the Southern Plains. Capitalists invested heavily in the cattle industry, and ranchers felt their fortunes were made.[34] But this climate was only temporary, and soon came the extreme weather—fire, droughts, and blizzards. Land became even more precious. Defending your finite grasslands from your competition's hungry cattle became a business necessity. As a result, big Texas ranchers had gone crazy for barbed wire; to them, this new technology meant security, prosperity, and property rights. The cattle weren't the only casualty; barbed wire was also killing off a way of life. The idea of the open range, that land and water belonged to all, was on its last breath. For the landless cowboys, the sheepherders, and the small landholders, this tool was choking off the land. They knew it as the "devil's rope."

For those who've spent time in and around rural Texas today, barbed wire is an often overlooked fact of life. Learning to navigate around it, and getting nicked by it, is part of growing up. But when the wire first came to Texas, it was so controversial that it led to what's called the Fence Cutter Wars: conflicts mainly between the big ranches and rag-tag associations of the dispossessed who opposed the privatization of the land on principle.

Over half of Texas counties were involved in some form of fence-cutting, with damages against the big-ranchers estimated at over $20 million.[35] It was a time when Texas cowboys joined together to take on private property.

Compared to agricultural traditions in the Northeast or Europe, fencing was limited in Texas before barbed wire. Particularly in the western part of Texas, where stone and solid wood were hard to come by, it made more sense to rely on the bountiful grassland to raise cattle rather than waste time and resources building a fence. This scarcity imposed a natural limit on how much a man could reasonably control; a paper claim might mean something in a court of law, but there was a physical limit to what a landowner could reasonably fence in. The open range was part of the commons, an idea that the land and water belonged to the people. But a boom in the cattle industry, propelled by speculation from Northern and European capitalists, put that system under strain. Barbed wire was cheap, and miles could be laid daily. Soon, many were blanketing their slice of grassland with the devil's rope. Indeed, large ranchers fenced so much land that they often cordoned off roads, schools, and waterways, which were public. In Archer County, Texas, the route to the courthouse was completely covered by barbed wire, rendering it impossible to reach the county seat without cutting a fence. In other cases, they'd fence over land that did not belong to them.[36] Ranchers who held land with rivers and creeks monopolized their hold on precious resources. Seeing what was coming, those who grazed their cattle upland of the enclosures argued that "the water should belong to all the land, since the rain which filled the streams fell on the whole plains region."[37]

This plea fell on deaf ears. It should come as no surprise that, as barbed wire won out against the open range, many ranches consolidated into the hands of a few large speculators, with little concern for what that meant for the other cowboys of the region.[38] By fencing in access to water, the big ranchers made the land upstream worthless—at which point they could swoop in to purchase it at a much lower price. Having fenced in much of the once public grassland, these land barons would continue to graze their cattle out on the open range until the grass had been chewed to dirt.

Who were these landlords and cattle barons? There were storybook characters of Texas legend, like Charles Goodnight, a man whose long list of achievements partially inspired the renowned novel *Lonesome Dove*.[39] But some of these new figures are likely less familiar, such as the Capitol Syndicate—previously mentioned in this book's introduction, which was granted 3 million acres of land by the State of Texas in exchange for constructing the Capitol in Austin—bringing together a bevy of investors inside and out of the state, including politicians like Illinois Senator Charles B. Farwell, and British capitalists like the Earl of Aberdeen.[40] The group founded the famous XIT Ranch on the Texas Panhandle, and were uninterested in working the land themselves but very interested in the money that came from it.

Fence-cutting was, at first, a practical measure. Landless cowboys were not doing anything new; they had always moved cattle from place to place. When they came across fencing, they would cut it, simple as that. Eventually, as the "devil's rope" spread across the plains, this individual action evolved into an organized project. Fence-cutters structured themselves into secret vigilante groups known as the Owls, the Javelinas, the Blue Devils, and the Knights of the Knippers. Come nightfall, they would rip and cut out the scourge of barbed wire as an act of protest, opening a new front in the class war against the land barons. Near San Antonio in Castroville, a rancher found a note ripped through with a bullet hole that read, "If you don't make gates, we will make them for you."[41] Another group in Live Oak County dug a grave and left a noose and a note, which said, "This will be your end if you rebuild this fence."[42] Another, on a Waco-area rancher's land, read:

> "You are ordered not to fence in the Jones tank, as it is a public tank and is the only water there for stock on this range. Until people can have time to build tanks and catch water, this should not be fenced. No good man will undertake to watch this fence, for the Owls will catch him. There is no more grass on this range than the stock can eat this year."[43]

Pasture burning and fence cutting went hand in hand. The landowners soon hired men to protect their fences. The pop of pistols firing echoed throughout the rural Texas night as each side tried to scare the other off.

While all this fencing and cutting was certainly a boon for the barbed wire producers, it had caused quite a political commotion. The legislature, of course, wanted to align with the landed elites. But there was a problem: The fence cutters had broad support among regular Texans. Anyone who aspired to have land for themselves, from small farmers to cowboys afraid of losing work, to the semi-large competitors of the largest cattle barons, joined in or silently supported the fence cutters. As one writer noted at the time, "Fence cutting never would have become so great and destructive if it had not met with such popular sentiment. Men of influence gave expression of favor. Many good men 'winked' at it until it had gone from the highest to the lowest. It found its way to the fireside of every home, and the greviences [sic] of the lawless element of the communistic fence-cutters were held up in glowing colors."[44] In 1884, Governor Ireland called a special session of the Texas legislature, where all kinds of denunciations of the anarchistic and communistic fence cutters were heard. A colorful legislator named Thomas Lawson Odom condemned the Fence Cutters as "the rag-tag and bob-tail and Hell-Hounds of Texas, no mercy should be shown to the midnight marauders."[45]

The legislature sided with the landowners and made fence cutting a felony punishable by five years; at the same time, they decreed that those who fenced in land that didn't belong to them was a simple misdemeanor.[46] Many questioned the fairness of the decision. "What!" exclaimed one newspaperman at the time. "Is the glory of Texas to be destroyed because the legislature refuses to legislate in favor of a section and a class?" He went on to invoke the Texas revolution: "not while the history of San Jacinto remains … shall it be said that Texas must be parcelled up because a few cattle kings are not permitted to … inclose and fence in lands not their own."[47]

The new felony charge kneecapped the broad communitarian activity among unorganized groups, though members of the clandestine fence-cutting gangs continued their crusade, albeit with less frequency. Drought and blizzards often resulted in flare-ups between fence cutters and cattle barons. The Texas Rangers were entrusted with enforcing the new laws on fence cutting, a charge they took with morbid pleasure. In the summer of 1888, Sergeant Ira Aten and Jim King were sent to Navarro County to crush fence cutting.[48] They posed as poor farmers, getting jobs as cotton pickers, and lived among the poor Texans, working next to them by day. By night, Jim King would play his fiddle to entertain his fellow pickers under the starry Texan sky.[49] But their friendly demeanor was a ruse, concealing a killer's intent. As they gained their fellow farmers' trust, they eventually found intel on the fence cutters, at which point Sergeant Aten began collecting dynamite. His intention was to rig the fences to explode when cut, blowing his newfound acquaintances to smithereens. So horrified were his superiors in Austin when they learned of their depravity, Aten and King were recalled, but the story had a chilling effect on fence cutters.[50] Considering the extent of the fence cutting and the cost incurred in the Fence Cutter War, it is surprising that there were so few deaths. Only three were recorded.[51]

* * *

One year after the big "Die-Up" of 1886, blizzards hit the Panhandle of Texas again. The plains were once more covered in mountains of frozen cattle.[52] The open range in Texas died with it. The cattle industry also went into crisis, as cattlemen across the Midwest flooded the market with cattle, with no care for quality or price. Suddenly, the seller's market for cattle collapsed. Texas cattlemen were lucky to sell for $10 per head, a nearly 66 percent decrease in price.[53]

The fence cutters' activities had forced Texans to, if not take sides, at least consider which side they were on. Whether or not you agreed with their acts of vandalism, it led people to consider the question of land in Texas. The railroad, barbed wire, and finance capital were flocking to Texas, leading to a change of life for all, from the cowboys in the Panhandle to the cotton farmers in Central Texas. The land question, and the question of labor versus capital, cut along racial lines, would combine to become the defining political conjuncture of the coming decades. One verbose but cutting letter in the *Galveston Daily News* got to the heart of the political question around land. Enraged by a previous letter that blamed the chaos around fence cutting on the "devilish spirit of communism in the country," one resident, writing under the pseudonym, "Rancho," responded:

> "The spirit of communism never maliciously cut a wire fence or perpetrated any other mischief by infringing upon the rights of any person in a wanton usurpation of authority arising from the power of wealth or money, and manifesting itself in the monopoly of the God-given heritage of the people and thus lay the foundations of a state of things in human society that forces its millions to starve, beg or steal... The demon I call agrarianism, aggressive greed on the part of a few wealthy monopolists, has done all this. It first moved the merciless money god to gobble up the lands, fence them, and thus virtually compel the small fish to get out of this murky

pool of strife made turbid by the foe of human happiness—selfishness, or be swallowed up."[54]

Without the disruptive effects of fencing, there would be no need for conflict. He proposed that the issue could be solved simply, through the creation of public land that the common people, "the real producers of wealth of the country," could share. Concluding, Rancho argued that this state of affairs was the most Christian and could lead Texas to educate itself and to reach a "more exalted moral plane," under this commonwealth:

> "For, every man being a law unto himself, distribution will be made to every man according to his necessities. And the bestowment will be directed in such manner as will conduce most to the good of the recipient, and will therefore prove a benediction to the giver—the people."[55]

The 'money-god' had come to Texas, and it wouldn't be satiated by the enclosure of the open range. Yet, contrary to popular belief, this new religion wasn't unanimously embraced. The fence cutters are but one piece of a vast Texas tradition of everyday people standing up against the abuses of the rich and powerful, even when the chance of victory is slim. The fight of the common people against its many onslaughts would soon take shape in the rise of Texas Populism.

Chapter 4

A Changing Texas

As Texas recovered from the devastation of the Civil War, a steady stream of people enticed by rumors of land and new opportunities flowed from east to west. After packing up their few, if any, belongings, Southerners would carve "G. T. T."—"Gone to Texas"—across the doors of their abandoned home, leaving the devastation and poverty behind. Soon, Texas would receive ever-growing "caravans of the poor—almost 100,000 every year of the 1870s,"[56] from the Old South. These new arrivals would try staking their claims in Texas, alongside Czech and German migrants, and would join in leading the uprisings of the poor to come.

It's worth dwelling for a moment on these caravans in particular. Much has been made of the "migrant caravans" that traveled from Southern Mexico to the U.S. border in recent years. There are many similarities between today's caravans traveling northward and the caravans traveling westward in the 1800s. As one observer of the exodus from the Old South into Texas wrote from Mississippi, "lines of emigrant wagons filled with hard-featured men and women bound for Texas and Arkansas."[57] In the coming story, these freshly arrived migrants will be known to us as Texans. Their impact on this state is undeniable, their authenticity unquestionable. As our current story is written, do we not extend the same courtesy to our neighbors?

These new migrants entered Texas and spread from the Panhandle, where Tascosa is located, to the Big Thicket, lining the state's eastern border with Louisiana.

But these sons and daughters of the "cotton States," as Northern journalist Edward King called them, fled one crisis to find another.[58] Between the growing power of the railroad companies and the rush of land speculation by (notably British and Northern) capitalists, land became harder to come by. Those who had it would see it pulled from under their feet. The aforementioned barbed wire and not-so-neighborly "improvements" on nearby properties were only some of the tactics employed to steal valuable land; so-called "land sharks" also used forgery, while newly anointed "cattle kings" let their "herds loose to destroy nesters' crops," and even poisoned small landholders' livestock.[59] The legal system, of course, was biased in favor of the rich and powerful.

Many farmers lost everything in these land grabs. However, it was the credit system that would prove to be the most devastating and long-lasting crisis facing rural Texans. Farmers were poor but needed supplies to grow cash crops like cotton, so they often relied on credit, using their crops as collateral—in what is often referred to as a crop-lien system. It was not uncommon for farmers to end up paying over a hundred percent markup on essential items, and in some instances, even higher than two hundred percent.[60] When the harvest finally came and farmers delivered their crop, usually cotton, to the merchant, they rarely met their balance, meaning it would carry over to the following year. And the next year. And the next.

Once this cycle began, it was nigh on impossible to get ahead of the debt. Fluctuating prices for crops like cotton only aggravated the farmers' misfortune. While farmers were buying at a premium, the furnishing merchants were able to buy most of their supplies at a steep discount wholesale from Northern suppliers.[61] The merchants owned the debt, but in many ways, they owned the debtors. If a farmer tried to take their business elsewhere, other merchants would refuse to offer them credit, the shop-owners' malevolent form of solidarity.[62]

The debts often grew to such an extent that the only way to get even with the merchants was to sell your land to pay the debt. But someone still needed to work the land. The number of tenant farmers, who had to provide rent to a landlord—usually through a portion of their crops, along with whatever else they owed the merchant—exponentially increased, while many long-time Texas farmers became tenants on land their family had once owned.[63] This was the system that farmers, white and black, lived under. It would define Texas politics for the generations to come.

Cotton, long the dominant crop in Texas, was still king, but its mandate in the international market was becoming more insecure from year to year, while improvements in technology and a population boom pushed the price down. However, it was often the crop that merchants and landlords required as payment. To make matters worse, Texas's population was one of the fastest-growing in the country—reaching nearly 1.6 million people in the 1870s[64]—and with it, cotton production nearly tripled, further lowering the price.[65] Farmers trying to avoid their financial obligations would only slide deeper into debt.

Meanwhile, the aforementioned merchants were making a killing on tenant farmers, and transporting cotton outside Texas was a burgeoning industry unto itself. Indeed, from the 1870s onward, the railroad industry boomed, with "27,000,000 acres to about 35,780,000 acres" of Texas handed out to the railroad companies, the new lords of the land.[66] This was largely because of the 1876 Constitution of Texas, which included land grants to railroad companies for each mile of track laid. The 1876 Constitution was a product of the backlash by Texas elites that would end Reconstruction and, with it, Republican rule, ushering in so-called "Redeemers" such as conservative Democrats like Governor Richard Coke, who was committed to restoring white supremacy in Texas. In turn, the railroads returned the favor to the people of Texas by jacking up transportation prices for everyone else.

New masters seemed to pop up everywhere and the indignity and anti-democratic spirit of the age would require radical and new solutions. In 1877, in Lampasas, Texas, a group of farmers gathered to discuss the many forces conspiring to keep them down. Together, they founded the Southern Farmers' Alliance, kicking off a slew of radical, people-powered movements that would not only shape the state of Texas but the entire nation for decades to come.

Chapter 5

Texas Populism, The Most Good For The Most People

Three million people would become members of the Farmers' Alliance, but it grew slowly in its early days.[67] It competed with The Grange, a national agricultural organization that promoted self-help and modern farming techniques and called for thrift and self-discipline. But what use is crop diversification when you are in debt? The massive land giveaways to the railroads had seen increases in poverty and tenant farming, lamented an article in the *Southern Mercury*, the official paper of the Farmers' Alliance, which:

> "cannot be attributed to lack of thrift on the part of the farmers, who are the wealth producers, because during the same period we increased the wealth in this country 100 per cent."[68]

Farmers recognized that, though they were poor, there was a lot of money being made off their labor. To win a better life would require more than thrift or the cult of individualism; it would take joining together. In direct contrast to groups like The Grange, the Farmers' Alliance organized around cooperation instead of competition. In its early days, the group set out to understand the political and economic reasons farmers were in peril, forming local chapters that provided a forum for folks to debate and investigate the issues they faced. The Alliance developed an understanding that merchants and buyers could ignore their individual demands, but collectively, farmers had the power to negotiate prices. To act on this insight, chapters established trade agreements with merchants, establishing exclusive deals to provide goods to Alliance members at a discount, based on the wholesale price. A similar system was set up for the selling of the farmers' products. In its first years, this strategy helped grow the Alliance and provided better conditions for a certain class of farmers. The strategy's effectiveness drew new members to the group; by joining the Alliance, farmers gained access to better pricing, but they also learned how acting collectively held the potential for benefits.

Still, this strategy was no silver bullet. Many tenant farmers and those indebted under the crop-lien system could not benefit from these trade agreements because they were for cash purchases only. This left out a significant portion of the poorest members of the Alliance.[69] Most farmers also had no way of knowing what the wholesale price of goods was, meaning they had to take merchants at their word. Last, the wholesalers, who sold goods to the middle-man merchants, did not approve of these trade agreements; ultimately, they put pressure on their middlemen to cease negotiations with the Farmers' Alliance.[70]

Another Alliance strategy was the formation of cooperative stores. This also had some success, until the merchant class and the wholesalers devised strategies to defeat them. Local merchants would collude with one another to keep prices lower than the cooperative store in order to force them out of business, and wholesalers would refuse to sell to cooperatives.[71] Additionally, Alliances formed cooperatively owned cotton gins, cottonseed oil mills, and corn mills. These, too, while helpful, could not fix the crisis in agriculture, specifically "the falling price of cotton."[72] One way to address this was called "bulking." The cotton industry was rife with middlemen. There were "twenty or so large exchanges" in the United States at the time, which sold to manufacturers and large buyers by the bale.[73] But to reach these exchanges, farmers had to either sell to their home merchant or to a "cotton factor," who purchased cotton from farmers and sold it to exchanges in bulk. This gave farmers very little leverage in price negotiation—that is, until they stored their own collective "bulks" of cotton together to negotiate for a higher price.[74] As some farmers began winning higher prices together, news spread fast, and these operations expanded across the state. But this tactic, like the others, could also come crashing down if a few farmers began accepting lower prices.[75] If farmers in one county stood together, merchants could traipse to the next county over and undermine the entire operation: As the Alliance discovered, "the only way an Alliance bulking strategy could work was to go beyond the local level."[76]

The difficulty of building cooperative alternatives did not dissuade membership in the Farmers' Alliance. If anything, it deepened the farmers' commitment to bolder approaches to the crisis of capitalism. Principles like solidarity took on a central importance, changing the way that people—neighbors—related with one another, and developing the political and economic ideas that later became part of the populist movement.

Though the Farmers' Alliance grew modestly in its first few years, it nearly faced collapse when it considered pursuing political independence too early. In 1874, Texas had returned to Democratic rule following the South's violent counterrevolution against Reconstruction. From then on, the Democratic Party dominated the state up until the end of the 20th century (for some perspective, that means Texas Democrats held majority power from the year the incandescent lamp was patented to the year *Forrest Gump* was released in theaters).

During this time, the ruling class of Texas was reasserting itself; there was little interest, from the powers that be, in cultivating the garden of democracy. Certain sections of the Farmers' Alliance tried to fuse the movement with the Greenback Party, a third-party movement consisting of a smattering of labor, farmers, and reform-minded people demanding anti-monopoly, anti-corruption, and monetary reforms. Some radical sections were prepared to carve out a farmer and labor alliance from the get-go, but they were in the minority. Many of the members of the Alliance were timid about directly taking on Texas's ruling class. Others were well-off enough that they did not share the class perspective of the poorer members of the Alliance. The internal conflict between the third-partyists and those who wanted to steer clear of politics led to the near collapse of the movement. Populism almost died in the cradle. The Farmers' Alliance had recognized the problems that farmers faced, but did it have an answer other than long meetings and contentious squabbles?

People began leaving the movement, and the Farmers' Alliance went from 120 to just 30 Alliance chapters by 1883.[77]

***

Faced with this terminal decline, the Farmers' Alliance acted boldly, creating a "Traveling Lecturer" position entrusted with advocating for the Alliance across Texas. S.O. Daws, a Mississippi-born son of the crop-lien system, filled the role. As a farmer, Daws had developed a keen understanding of the problem. "There is something radically wrong somewhere when those who work most get least, and those who work least get most," he co-wrote in 1887 with Alliance President W.L. Garvin. "This fact forces itself home to every thoughtful mind. We want to find where that wrong is. Therefore, we must organize."[78]:

> And organize they did. With Daws, the Alliance found not only a champion of the Alliance but also a theorist with an understanding of class power. As a speaker, Daws was undoubtedly capable of reflecting on the severity of the abuses farmers like him faced, but what drew crowds to hear Daws speak was his capacity to point people toward solutions. The solution, of course, was to join the Farmers' Alliance—and the people did. The 1883 convention had seen only 30 delegates, but by 1885, over 600 were in attendance. The Alliance even had to limit how many delegates each local could send to their convention.[79]

The Texas Populist movement was filled with characters larger than life. People like H.S.P. "Stump" Ashby, who, of course, held many of the typical former professions of an Allianceman—Confederate soldier, farmer, and cowboy—and many unexpected ones, such as a stint travelling as a circus clown.[80] Another, J.H. "Cyclone" Davis, in a debate with a Democrat in Kentucky, drew from the Bible and the pantheon of American political thought, leaving his opponents speechless. A press report covering the event called him a "cyclone from Texas," which is how he'd earned his nickname—and a commission to speak on behalf of the Farmers' Alliance across the country.[81] "When God said, 'If any man will not work, neither shall he eat,' he meant to dignify labor," Davis once said. "This and another divine declaration, 'In the sweat of thy face shalt thou eat bread,' have been ignored in all ages and labor made a serf."[82] S.O. Daws also had a protege who he had hired as a traveling lecturer, William Lamb, a Tennessean turned Texan with little to no formal education. Lamb would later achieve what the early movement had failed to do: transform the farmers' revolt from a protest organization into a political party capable of shaking the nation.

Alliance speakers were unmatched as showmen and as agitators. They spoke not only to farmers' immediate concerns but also to the problems of capitalism and of a government that worked on behalf of the rich. They knew how to grow a crowd, how to lambast the enemies of the farmer legislating in Austin. And when people asked how to fight back, the answer was simple: Well, join the Alliance! This army of paid speakers spread the populist dream across Texas, and in short order, across the South and Midwest. As the Alliance grew, members would hold "encampments" where people would revel for days with fiery populist speakers about the evils of capitalism and the righteousness of the Alliance.

These encampments were no small affairs. Folks ate well and danced into the evening. An 1891 event in Sulphur Springs, Texas, was covered on the front page of *The Fort Worth Gazette*: "the 'encampment' which opened here to-day promises to be the greatest coming together of people—laboring people—that was ever witnessed in this portion of Texas."[83] Estimates put the event at 8,000 to 10,000. Numbers like these should come as a shock to anyone who has ever organized a political rally, where attendance in the dozens can be seen as a success, to say nothing of hundreds or thousands. These gatherings not only brought opportunity to spread populist ideas, they gave members the confidence to stand up against their opponents.[84] Rhetorical appeals to "the people," whether in speech or in print, are effective, but nothing will convince you of the strength of your movement like the sight of thousands who share your goal.

Social life was critical to the success of the Farmers' Alliance, providing meaning and purpose. Its summer encampments, dances, and barbecues brought people together and allowed members to form friendships that politics—no matter how righteous—cannot. Class politics, at its heart, is the recognition that there are others who share your interests and needs, and that by working together, those needs can be met. And while abstract principles are important, alongside calls for solidarity with the people and the working-class, it is even better when you know the names of those you are standing with. It is the expansion of the self, of your hopes and dreams, stretching one's sense of justice, beyond one person's creature comforts, to having right done to your neighbors, to your neighbors' neighbors, and so on. As the great historian Lawrence Goodwyn notes, "The farmers of the Alliance had spent much of their lives in humiliating circumstances… they were ridiculed for their poverty, and they knew it."[85] But by joining together, "they had found something new. That something may be described as individual self-respect and collective self-confidence, or what some would call 'class-consciousness.'" [86]

Farmers took this self-respect seriously. Self-education in economics, history, and politics was encouraged by Alliance members, demonstrating a confidence in the capacity of everyday people to understand the world around them and their interest in putting in the work to understand. Moreover, education produced more active members. Alliance meetings and encampments were the sites of serious debate, not passive head nodding. This is something that political organizations today would do well to note. As one farmer wrote at the time in *The Rural Citizen*:

> "Methinks I see a grand future for the Alliance. The people have become convinced that there is something wrong with the machinery of the government and they are studying to find a remedy for the wrongs."[87]

History was happening, and by joining the Farmers' Alliance, you could participate in it. The common people were being mistreated but something could be done about it. Even more radically, the populists believed that the common people should be the ones to act and to rule. This belief in the ability of everyday people is the democratic heart of populism. As the 20th-century socialist C.L.R. James once wrote, "Every cook can govern."[88]

* * *

The Alliance continued to grow and, in 1886, found itself engaged in the fundamental political question: Which side are you on? The Knights of Labor, an early American labor organization, had helped orchestrate a railroad workers' strike against the Texas and Pacific Railway owned by the financier Jay Gould. The legendary labor leader Martin Irons had called for the action after the firing of union leaders in Marshall, Texas.[89] When the Knights asked the Farmers' Alliance to join in a boycott of the railways, the red-haired and red-blooded William Lamb challenged the Alliance to see itself in common struggle with all "plain" and working people.

In a thunderous letter to the Alliance membership, Lamb wrote, "We think all members should show the world which side they are on."[90] In this letter, the Texan radical Lamb lays out the case for solidarity. Connecting the farmers' plight to that of the railroad workers was a critical development in the coming populist revolt. And while certainly coming from a deep sense of moral clarity, Lamb made the case based on the shared interests of the class: "Knowing that the day is not far distant when the Farmer's Alliance will have to use the boycott on manufacturers.... We think it is a good time to help the Knights of Labor in order to secure their help in the future."[91] As Lawrence Goodwyn wrote, "Populism—began with this letter."[92] This is not just one of the founding documents of Populism; it is one of the founding documents of political and labor solidarity in the United States. And it was written in Texas.

Not all Alliance leadership agreed. Lamb's letter was directed at the Alliance state president, Andrew Dunlap, and the editor of *The Rural Citizen*, J.N. Rogers, who had called boycotts the work of "busy bodies in other men's business."[93] This would open a rift within the Farmers' Alliance between a conservative faction advocating for the organization to stay out of politics and a radical faction aimed at uniting the working class and pursuing independent political power. Lamb, who had publicly called for a boycott before writing his letter, was rebuffed by President Dunlap, who claimed Lamb had no authority to make such a call.[94] Dunlap was probably correct procedurally, but Lamb, in his day-to-day work in the Alliance, was closer to and had a better sense of rank-and-file sentiments. The Knights of Labor took on the robber barons, and while they were up against a formidable foe, they never went hungry. Gould attempted to starve out the strikers by denying them pay, but the farmers of Texas thwarted him. Throughout the fight, Texas farmers—including Farmers' Alliance members—delivered food to the striking workers. The Alliancemen saw Jay Gould as an enemy of the working class, and in the Knights of Labor, they saw brothers. [95]

The same year, this connection between the plight of farmers and industrial workers made its way into another foundational document of American and Texan history, the Cleburne Demands of 1886. With this list of demands addressed to the government of Texas and the United States, the Farmers' Alliance was no longer just an association of farmers, but a political organization that intended to speak and be heard—a fundamental shift in the history of populism. The demands begin:

"We, the delegates to the Grand State Farmer's Alliance of Texas... demand of our state and national governments ... legislation as shall secure to our people freedom from the onerous and shameful abuses that the industrial classes are now suffering at the hands of arrogant capitalists and powerful corporations."[96]

Gone was the traditional language of rural revolt, of conflict between town and country. Here, instead, were bold and explicit condemnations of arrogant capitalists and powerful corporations. Following the spirit of William Lamb's impassioned plea, the farmers now saw themselves not just as allies of the union movement but as members of the same class—the working class.

The demands should be considered the founding documents of the progressive and the American socialist movement. The first demand was for recognition of "trade unions," but also "cooperative stores" and other collective organizations of the working class. Other demands put forward by the farmers included taxes on land speculation and a requirement that "railroad property shall be assessed at the nominal value of the stock on which the railroad seeks to declare a dividend."[97] It also included a demand to end convict labor in the state of Texas, that the state ensure corporations pay their taxes and their workers "according to their contract," and that workers would get the first opportunity to purchase what they produced.

The Cleburne Demands had specific planks to address the accumulation of land by foreign—primarily English and Scottish—syndicates. One plank directly called for the state to force the sale of the land owned by these financial interests to "actual settlers." Plank 7 of the demands also called for the forced removal of unlawful barbed wire fences across the state, which cattle barons had used to seize Texans' land.

The ruling classes in Texas had organized themselves into trade associations that wielded tremendous power over the prices people paid and the conditions workers faced. Why should the toiling classes not do the same? The Farmers' Alliance had sparked a consciousness amongst Texas farmers beyond its agricultural roots. It united with a growing, more powerful, and militant labor movement. As S.O. Daws said, "Capital is thoroughly organized, but when the laboring class begins to organize, they call it communism and other hard names."[98] The red-baiting of the farmers, all the way back in the 1880s, is a common theme in Texan and American politics and always seems to occur when regular people start asking, why do those "who work most get least, and those who work least get most?"

* * *

Along with the Cleburne Demands, another idea that would be central to Populism was being developed. Dr. Charles William Macune had moved around like many other members of the Farmers' Alliance. Unlike them, however, he had seen success after success. Born in Wisconsin, he moved to California and Kansas before finally settling in Texas in 1870.[99] A lawyer, doctor, newspaperman, and farmer, Macune was a great leader of the Farmers' Alliance. As a staunch Democrat, he would not join the radicals in their new party when the time came. But he would give the farmers a great gift in advocating for what's known as the Subtreasury Plan—soon to become the programmatic backbone of the Farmers' Alliance and the People's Party—which hoped to address issues of money scarcity, falling agricultural prices, and the usurious crop-lien system all at once.

The 1880s saw a monetary crisis in Texas and practically everywhere else—due partly to the gold standard and other global economic factors—which especially harmed farmers, since they needed to borrow money at the beginning of each growing season. It also led to falling prices in agricultural goods, meaning farmers would make less at the end of the season while their debts increased in value in real terms, making it all but impossible for farmers to get ahead of debt. In response, farmers wanted to expand the money supply. One plan popular among populists, sometimes called free silver, was to mint money backed by plentiful silver. But Macune's Subtreasury Plan, while slightly complicated, was more holistic in scope.

Essentially, it called for the federal government to establish smaller treasuries—subtreasuries—across the United States, "alongside warehouses and elevators in which farmers could store certain nonperishable commodities" such as cotton and wheat.[100] In return, farmers would receive a treasury note of up to eighty percent of the stored crops' value, with an interest rate of one percent. Farmers could retrieve their crops to sell from the warehouses at any time.[101] This system would allow farmers to hold out on selling their crops until they were able to receive a reasonable price. Under the system of the day, if a farmer needed cash to pay off their debts, they were at the mercy of the buyers; but under the Subtreasury Plan, if a farmer was desperate for cash, they could borrow against their crops stored in the subtreasury warehouse, pay off their debts, and sell their crops at the best possible price. It was a brilliant solution to the issues farmers faced, which the government would back. Decades later, during the New Deal, another system built off the Subtreasury

Plan would allow farmers to receive government loans based on their land, under similarly favorable terms.[102] These loans were paid out by the Subtreasury in "legal tender, treasury notes, or greenbacks," providing a fiat money supply in the United States, and taking the country off of the gold standard, or limiting the cruelty of what Populists called the "money-power."[103]

It would take political power to implement Macune's Subtreasury Plan, but the Farmers' Alliance was split on how to relate to political power. Should the group involve itself in electoral squabbles, or focus wholly on economic issues? Was it worth reforming the Democratic Party, or creating a third-party from scratch? While the conservative side of the movement still held institutional power, William Lamb and other radicals were growing in strength—and they wanted to push the Alliance in a more political direction. In the 1886 convention in Cleburne, the radicals replaced *The Rural Citizen* with the much more radical *Dallas Mercury*, which soon changed its name to *Southern Mercury*. The conservatives feared exposing the full extent of the gulf between the leadership and the base of the movement, and this change went through with little resistance.

The change of newspaper proved decisive in cementing the more radical direction for the movement. Just a few years later, it would regularly print biting criticism of the status quo in Texas and demand that working people unite to change it.

"There is not, never was, indeed never can be any legitimate conflict between the interests of capital and labor. There always has been a bitter and irrepressible conflict between the capitalist and the laborer, and this relentless struggle will continue as long as wage labor exists, because the capitalist always seeks to enslave the laborer by preying upon his earnings; and as long as men desire justice and freedom, the war will go on till the system is abolished. Chattel slavery had its days. It ran its course till under the glare of the increasing intelligence it tottered to its grave amid the din, roar and smoke of civil war. It is to be hoped that wage slavery will find an early grave in this country through the medium of the ballot box."[104]

This piece, published in 1892, identifies not just the crop-lien system, the credit issue, or even merely the political influence of the railroads as the cause of farmers' plight, but rather an intractable conflict between "capital and labor." It also, in the spirit of Alliance radical William Lamb, fuses the plight of the farmers to the plight of the entire working class; in fact, it makes no distinction between the two. The defiant tone captured the mood of the radical wing of the Alliancemen after a failed attempt to coerce the Democratic Party into meaningful action. And political independence was being demanded, in Alliance meetings and the pages of the *Southern Mercury*.

After years of attempting to reform the Democratic Party, members were exhausted with all of its betrayals. As a farmer, J.Z. Greene wrote in the paper:

"When you are laboring side by side with your wife and daughter and see your children developing into manhood and womanhood with minds uncultured and bodies deformed from labor, ask yourself if you live in a free country. If you are desperately in love with either of the two political parties, could you give us the reason? ... Is it because they gave away enough of our public lands to make empires and caused one-fourth of American farmers to become tenants for their lords?"[105]

This sentiment was put even more succinctly by Mrs. Bettie Gay from Columbus, Texas: "I read in a book the other day where a man said he would vote for an ox if nominated on the old democratic ticket. Shades of Caesar! Whither are we drifting?"[106]

The *Southern Mercury* would play an influential role in shaping the consciousness of populists not just in Texas but across the country. While the conflict around political independence continued under the surface, the Farmers' Alliance would play a major role in influencing the Democratic Party, particularly through its support of the reform wing.

Chapter 6

Hogg, The Failures of Reform, and The People's Party

James Hogg, the first native-born governor of Texas, was born on March 24, 1851, in Cherokee County, around 100 miles southeast of Dallas. Weighing in at over 300 pounds, Hogg, a skilled politician, was known for his size—and the unfortunate decision to name his daughter Ima; as in, Ima Hogg. He's also famous for his appetite: Hogg once claimed he could not bear to "see the spare-ribs, back-bones, sausages, chitlings and sauce, spoil."[107] But he should be better known for representing the end of Redeemer Democrats' power in Texas. His tenure as governor also doubles as a kind of allegory for radical movements such as the Farmers' Alliance: Just because you set the table doesn't mean you're invited to the meal.

Texans were angry that the Austin government had given away so much land to the railroad companies. James Hogg played well with the angry mood of the day, publicly aligning himself with a coalition of farmers and laborers. His previous success as a reform-minded Attorney General, critical of the power of the large landowners and railroads, provided him with enough bona fides to win the support of many of the state's insurgent labor and farmer organizations.[108] Running as a changemaker against the Democratic establishment, he specifically rallied Texans against the railroads and "corporate power." In his opening speech in his 1890 gubernatorial run at Rusk, Texas, Hogg warned that failure to enact regulations on the railroads would lead to revolution, leaving the country unable to "restrain the commune," or "suppress the anarchist," adding, "[t]he issue so sharply drawn in the present campaign is, shall corporate power or the State control? The fight is on."[109] As a labor leader at the time wrote, "You can see we had our eye on the gun when we nominated Hogg for Governor against the money power of the state."[110]

However, while Hogg was willing to address concerns about railroad regulation, he was staunchly opposed to the most precious question for reform-minded Alliancemen, the Subtreasury Plan. For leaders like William Lamb who believed it was time for a new party, this was unacceptable. Hogg was the Democrats' answer to the needs of the farmers, who had grown in power and influence through the Southern Farmers' Alliance. What kind of answer would he be if he were willing to talk about the plight of the farmers and corporate power, but opposed their solution? Even worse, Lamb feared what would happen to the momentum of the Farmers' Alliance if they were so easily brought back into the "party of their fathers." But Lamb, with years of experience in Alliance politics, knew how to politicize an issue. At the August state convention for the Texas Alliance, he pushed the organization to endorse the Subtreasury as a formal plank of the movement, knowing full well that the Texas Democratic Party had officially opposed it in their convention. The organization voted in favor with seventy-five counties voting "yes," twenty-three voting "no" and sixteen abstentions.[111] The Alliance was officially in conflict with the Democrats, who had shown they were willing to offer crumbs from the reform movement, but would leave the power of the merchant class and the crop-lien untouched. With no serious challengers, Hogg was set to become governor and benefited immensely from the support of rank-and-file union members and Alliancemen. He made the right enemies among the rich—Jay Gould, for instance, told the *Dallas Morning News* that there would be less interest in investing in the state due to regulations, and he cancelled a railroad project due to "the prospect of hostile legislation."[112] But Hogg withstood the pressure, and the Farmers' Alliance had played a key role in securing his nomination by threatening through its papers to field their own candidate if Hogg were not nominated.[113] The move worked, establishing the Alliance as a potent force in the Democratic Party. But Lamb's tactics enabled the Alliance to capitalize on the reform-minded energy surrounding Hogg's election while laying the groundwork for political independence.

In many ways, Hogg would prove to be a sharp break from the politics of his predecessors in the Democratic Party, marking the beginning of a new era in Texas politics. Where lobbying for railroad regulation had once been slow-going for the Alliance, Hogg made it one of his key issues. Once in office, he established the Texas Railroad Commission, as Alliancemen had demanded, much to the robber barons' chagrin. Indeed, Hogg added many of the Alliance's demands to his platform, and where his platform differed, as political scientist Roscoe Martin notes, it often went *even further* than what Alliance members had hoped. Hogg's platform, for instance, called for "the abolition of the national banking system and [...] for the free and unlimited coining of silver."[114] He also addressed many of the concerns outlined in the Cleburne Demands, and the legislature passed "an alien land law aimed at foreign syndicates, and laws regulating public and railway securities, increasing educational funds, and abolishing the convict lease."[115] Though the question of the Subtreasury still lingered, it seemed as if the debate of reform of the Democratic Party versus political independence was settled.

It did not take long for relations to sour. Though Hogg had established the Texas Railroad Commission per the Alliance's request, he soon betrayed the movement by appointing the board himself and not choosing any Alliancemen for the commission.[116] Indeed, this was the first of many snubs; James Hogg and the Democratic Party outmaneuvered the radicals at nearly every turn. Next, the Subtreasury Plan, key to the Alliance's appeal to empower farmers, came under criticism from Democrats, including Alliance members of the Texas Legislature. The timing was strange. Why, shortly after winning a sweeping election, would Hogg, Democrats, and conservative Alliancemen turn so quickly on their coalition members? Whether Hogg had decided it was best to handle the disagreement in an "off-season" or anticipated that the Alliance would become a "thorn in his flesh" by the next election, it is likely that these attacks were ordered by Governor Hogg himself.[117]

The disagreement was so bad that a lawmaker and an Alliance legislative committee member smacked each other around in the Texas Capitol.[118] In March 1891, rightwing Alliance legislators came together and released what is known as the "Austin Manifesto," claiming that the officially non-partisan Farmers' Alliance intended to make itself into a political organization "and ally it with the incipient third party."[119] Hogg, having won the election and enjoying firm control of his party, had seized the opportunity to neutralize the farmers' popular demands. The State Democratic Chairman, N.W. Finley, in an order to Democrats, called the Alliance a "treacherous enemy" and ordered Democrats to refuse them entrance in "democratic councils and in Democratic primaries."[120] For their part, the right-wing Alliancemen in Austin attempted to create a new Farmers' Alliance—the "Grand State Farmers' Alliance."[121] This one would not support the Subtreasury Plan, nor would it have many members.

The pretenders were widely ridiculed. In the *Southern Mercury,* a piece entitled "Fort Worth Scab Alliance(?) Meeting" ran with the following: "They met, they did! The Hogg-Dixon Scab Gang! Thirty-seven all told!"[122] Hogg's betrayal of the Alliance, supported by the movement's conservative faction, provided William Lamb and his allies all the justification needed to move the organization in a new direction. They began charting the new path for the populist movement—an alliance between farmers and labor—and political independence.

* * *

In early spring 1891, William Lamb, Bill Farmer, and "Stump" Ashby encouraged members of the Alliance to send members to

51

the founding convention of the People's Party in Cincinnati.[123] A group of Texans made the trip and, along with mostly Midwestern farmers, organized the populist movement into the People's Party. Shortly after, in August of 1891, William Lamb chaired the first Texas convention of the People's Party in Dallas. Since his early advocacy in the Farmers' Alliance, Lamb had long been a leader in pushing for an alternative to the Democratic Party. Finally, after years of work, William Lamb would gavel in the meeting and forever change Texas.

The party's platform was rooted in the immediate needs of Texans but had an eye for the larger issues affecting farmers. It also saw itself as part of an international movement, claiming the formation of the People's Party was a response to "the great social, industrial and economic revolution now dawning upon the civilized world."[124] Calling for "radical reforms" to combat the abuses by leaders of the Republican and Democratic parties that had "fastened a system of finance on the Nation which is sapping the vitals of our institutions and enslaving our people."[125] In their words, the United States Senate had become a "den of millionaires," and Texas's government was no better, "stealing the guise of heaven in which to serve the purpose of hades, they have, … squandered almost all the available public domain the heritage of the people of this and future generation."[126]

To combat this, the populists demanded reform of the monetary system, which was making it near impossible for the indebted to get ahead (chief among the reforms was "the free and unlimited coinage of silver").[127] Many of their other proposals rhyme with progressive movements today: Guarantees for education, including free textbooks; an end to convict labor; and the direct election of the president and U.S. Senators through a "secret ballot." They also called for laws barring the foreign ownership of land, and for Congress to reclaim the land owned by "foreign syndicates," which would force the railroads and other corporations to release the land that they were not using to the people. Moreover, they demanded that communication and transportation be put under public control, for the benefit of all. The coalition between labor and farmers is apparent in the demands for a "more equitable ... lien law," the eight-hour working day, and requirements that railroads pay their employees in real money.[128]

In the early days, Texas Democrats did the fledgling People's Party plenty of favors. By waging war on the Subtreasury Plan and banning Alliancemen from Democratic primaries, Democrats made the choice clear: Abandon all of the principles of the Farmers' Alliance, or join the People's Party. Some holdouts were reluctant to leave the Democratic fold. Texas, since its admittance into the union, had been governed by Democrats, save for a few short interruptions: under Sam Houston, who opposed secession and held the governorship until 1861—the outbreak of the Civil War—and during Reconstruction, when Republican E.J. Davis was in charge. Even as the conflict between Populism and the Democratic Party worsened, a few Alliancemen were still hesitant. A short-lived movement of "Jeffersonian Democrats," mainly Alliancemen angry at Democratic leadership but unwilling to accept the split, produced a platform almost identical to the People's Party and called for continued organizing within the local Democratic Party.[129] But most of these men found their way into the People's Party once the Farmers' Alliance on a national level threw their support behind it.

Hope that Hogg represented a change in Texas politics in a progressive direction was dashed. He was interested in reorienting politics in Texas, but he wanted politics to revolve around himself. He was not the first, nor the last, Southern governor to appeal to the people on the stump and betray them in office. His politicking was fitting of a character who would go on to co-found The Texas Company, better known as Texaco.

To take on Hogg's political machine in the 1892 election, the People's Party nominated Thomas L. Nugent, a temperate former Democratic judge who had left the party in 1889, and had long aligned himself with reform movements. In his run for governor, he was able to trace his bona fides all the way back to Texas's 1875 constitutional convention where, as a delegate, he had opposed the handouts to the railroads.[130] He was soft-spoken but committed to his political beliefs; What he lacked in fiery speech was more than made up for by his compelling and logical presentation of the great moral and economic crises Texas faced.[131]

As a member of the Swedenborgian church, Nugent believed "that Jesus had been an incarnation of God himself," to guide man to become "the kind of being God wished them to become."[132] His beliefs were inseparable from his politics. Nugent believed the life of Jesus Christ was the "beginning of Christian socialism," and that Jesus was brought "into the human world to transform and uplift and glorify the social man[.]"[133] This gospel-infused socialism would be a mainstay of Texas Populism and the coming American socialist movement. You can hear the echoes of Nugent in Eugene Debs, or in the speeches of Norman Thomas, and the early teachings at Commonwealth College, the radical socialist school in Arkansas.[134]

This spirit can be felt in a speech Thomas Nugent delivered in 1894 in Grand View, Texas, to a meeting of the State Farmers' Alliance on the evils of "plutocratic capitalism":

"It gathers the fruits of industry and divides them at its will. It controls and manipulates with almost unbridled power and license every function of trade and finance. Its speculative lust finds opportunities of gain in tolls levied upon the right to occupy the earth. It denies to the people the heritage which the Creator gave them 'without money and without price.' It gathers into its storehouse the bounties which nature designed for the common use of all... It robs genius of its glory, makes of intellect a drudge and a slave, and utilizes the achievements of science to raid the stock markets and enlarge the margin of profits. Thus it wipes out as with a sponge the distinction between right and wrong, makes merchandise of the noblest ideals, sets gain before the world as the highest end of life, and converts men into predatory human animals."[135]

Nugent's dissection of the changes that capitalism was bringing to Texas echoed similar ones made by Karl Marx, minus the religious convictions, nearly fifty years before: "All that is solid melts into air, all that is holy is profaned, and man is at last compelled to face with sober senses his real conditions of life, and his relations with his kind."[136] Through the efforts of visionaries like William Lamb, "Stump" Ashby, and Bill Farmer, populism found its voice. Through Charles Macune's Subtreasury it found its head. Through the People's Party, the movement found its feet. And through Thomas L. Nugent, populism found its soul.

Nugent and the Populists' 1892 campaign focused on economic issues. For farmers, and to a lesser extent laborers, the focus on the monetary crisis via coinage of silver and railing against the usurious loans system provided plenty of reason to support them. The Democrats' war on the Subtreasury Plan spurred support from Alliancemen for personal benefit, and the added chance to spite the leaders who'd scorned them. The People's Party's commitment to addressing abuses by the railroads against Texans—including abuses against railway workers—along with their endorsement of the eight-hour workday, brought support from members of the Knights of Labor, who remembered the solidarity the Farmers' Alliance had shown labor in their time of need.

On the other side of the aisle, Governor Hogg's decision to put regulations on the railroads had made him powerful enemies. The conservative Democrats revolted against Hogg, rallying around a company man, the railroad lawyer George Clark, who ran an independent campaign for governor.[137] While a split in the Democratic Party could've benefitted the Populists, it also created a "spoiler dilemma": The fear that a vote for Nugent could lead to the dismantling of the progress achieved under Hogg.[138] Of principal concern was the railroad commission; the railroad interests backed Clark and would certainly destroy it if elected. The Republican Party also supported Clark and did not run a candidate in the election, making the threat of a spoiler real.[139] In the end, Clark's inclusion in the race, and the fear that supporting this new third party could lead to a right-wing Democrat victory, led many potential Populist voters to stick with Hogg.[140] In the end, Hogg won 43.7 percent of the vote, with Clark more than 13 points behind him. In third, with nearly 25 percent of the vote, was Thomas Nugent, an impressive feat given the relative youth of the People's Party.[141]

The downballot results were also promising. People's Party candidates won eight state representative seats and one in the state senate.[142] Despite the fact that Populist candidates tended to skew slightly older than the average Democrat politician, young voters in Texas—who felt the American Dream wasn't in the cards for them—greatly preferred the Populists over the Democrats.[143] As historians Worth Robert Miller and Stacy G. Ulbig have shown, the populist successes in 1892 "owed… a lot to their origins in the Southern Farmers' Alliance and the Knights of Labor," with Populist votes strongly correlating with the presence of the Farmers' Alliance and Knights of Labor chapters, though correlation with the presence of a Farmer's Alliance chapter was somewhat weaker.[144] Meanwhile, Matthew Hild, in his investigation of the role of the Knights of Labor in Texas's third party movement, has shown, "Nugent carried several counties that either were then or recently had been centers of Knights of Labor strength, such as Comanche, Delta, Erath, Lampasas, Navarro, Palo Pinto, and Titus."[145] A potential labor-farmer coalition was proving to be a real possibility in Texas. But to be successful, the movement needed to do more.

Fundraising was a major hurdle for the organization.[146] And while Populism had powerful speakers and a vibrant press, its media reach was outnumbered by a hostile and pro-Democrat media. The Populists "did best among white southern-born farmers"; these were not "planters, but instead sleeveless poor whites from poorer soil regions."[147] The Populists had done well with this base, but black voters, apart from a few notable exceptions, did not go populist. In fact, they had gone for Hogg.[148]

Chapter 7

"A Battlefield In Which Many Errors Have Been Made In The Past"

Populism would have a difficult relationship with race, to put it lightly. The Farmers' Alliance had barred black membership in the organization, limiting its reach across the state, especially in the "Old South" regions of East Texas. Radicals understood this exclusion would hamper the movement. Shortly after the Cleburne Demands of 1886, a Colored Alliance formed and grew to more than a million members nationally.[149] Like the white Farmers' Alliance, this organization had its heart in Texas with Houston County serving as an "institutional base of the Colored National Farmers' Alliance."[150] Black people had been deeply involved in the stirrings that led to the populist revolt. The Greenback Party movement, which preceded the People's Party, had "eight or ten" black people among the "forty delegates," in Austin in 1878. The fact that the convention had a plank protecting the rights of people regardless of "race, color or creed," and the fact that the movement's first newspaper, the *National View*, had an article by Frederick Douglass urging black people to stay in the South instead of moving North, is a testament to the deep involvement of black members of the early third party movement.[151] But for whites in the Farmers' Alliance, challenging the South's racist regime was not a straight line.

You would be mistaken to consider the Colored Farmers' Alliance as a simple offshoot of the Farmers' Alliance. While it had support from radical members of the Farmers' Alliance like William Lamb and "Stump" Ashby, and was engaged in similar work, the Colored Alliance was a distinct organization. It shared many of the priorities with the white Farmers' Alliance, but it also had its own. With an estimated membership of a million members, this was no auxiliary organization. For example, at the Alliance convention in Ocala, Florida, the Colored Alliance and the Farmers' Alliance differed on what was called the "force bill." Congressman Henry Cabot Lodge of Massachusetts had put forward a bill calling for federally run elections—a threat to the Democratic machines that ran the South, which used all kinds of intimidation and dubious tactics to ensure they remained on top. Southern Democratic Party newspapers heavily vilified the law. The specter of federal troops reoccupying the South was effective, and the white Farmers' Alliance in Ocala condemned the plan, while the Colored Farmers' Alliance endorsed the law.[152] Another example of the Colored Alliance taking the agrarian revolt further than their white counterparts was in their 1890 national convention: "land is not property, can never be made property," affirmed the Colored Farmers' Alliance delegates, adding, "The land belongs to the sovereign people."[153]

In addition to the economic villains and degradation of the crop-lien system, the Colored Alliance contended with threats from white mobs, the police, and a hostile government. Due to threats of violence, the Colored Alliance operated in a more clandestine fashion.[154] As Lawrence Goodwyn noted, "There could be no vast Colored Alliance cooperatives, and no public demonstrations of support for the cooperatives, no wagon trains stretching for miles, no spectacular summer encampments."[155] This is not to say that the movement was invisible. Across the South, hundreds of thousands would call themselves members, and a generation of black political agrarian leaders would be cultivated within the Colored Alliance. Men like J.J. Shuffer and H.S. Spencer would help ensure that the Colored Farmers' Alliance would thrive.[156]

Among these members was the white R.M. Humphrey, a Confederate veteran from South Carolina, a Baptist minister, and the man whose farm hosted the founding meeting of the Colored Farmers' Alliance.[157] He was appointed as the honorary "Superintendent" of the organization and became one of its lead spokespeople. Humphrey was also present at the grand meetings that would bring many of the members of the Colored Farmers' Alliance into the People's Party.[158]

At the beginning of the populist movement, the Republican Party was most black Texans' political home. Democrats thoroughly controlled the state after Reconstruction, and Republicans were unable to compete on a state level. They fared better on the county level, in communities with large black populations; from there, Republicans were able to hold many local positions and send representatives to the Texas Legislature.[159] This foothold in power provided material benefits—jobs, stability—to black Texan communities.[160] But after Reconstruction crumbled, the Republican Party nationally was a party of business, no longer interested in fighting for black people's civil rights. White

Republicans in Texas were hoping to shed the party of its black constituency. Across Texas, so-called Lily-white Republican clubs, intended to limit black people's role in the Republican Party, sprang up like weeds. (Among their membership was none other than the son of the Texas hero and unionist Sam Houston.)[161] As one member of the aligned Republican White League of Texas put it, "The union is only safe in the hands of the Anglo-Saxon race, and that a Republican party in Texas to merit the respect of mankind must be in the hands of that race."[162] The Lily-whites were rebelling against what they saw as the unsafe hands of Norris Wright Cuney, a Galveston-area politician and early civil rights leader whose mother, Adeline Stuart had been enslaved by his white planter father Philip Minor Cuney.[163] This conflict between the Lily-white faction and the Cuney wing opened an opportunity for the populists to gain the support of black voters.

Black Texans' support for Republicans wasn't out of blind loyalty. With twenty-two percent of the population, they could be decisive in a close election.[164] As a black delegate told members at the first Populist convention in 1891, "The negro vote will be the balancing vote in Texas," and "if you are going to win, you will have to take the negro with you."[165] Much of Jim Crow order "had yet to be erected in 1890." While segregation had spread through the founding of separate organizations and churches, this was not mandated by law, save for "public schools ... and a controversial railroad-car segregation law."[166] The limits on voting that would affect black people were yet to fully ossify within Texas institutions. The Populists had an opening. The results of 1892 showed there was more work to be done.[167]

Following the election, "Stump" Ashby understood that work would mean relying on travelling lecturers, decrying the abuses of the Democratic Party, and turning the disaffected into upstanding populists. Ashby was lucky to have two great black populists with him, John B. Rayner and Melvin Wade.[168] Similar to the Farmers' Alliance's move to hire S.O. Daws, the People's Party's decision to bring these men on would reignite the People's Party.

John B. Rayner, a short man who still possessed a towering presence, was born a slave in North Carolina in 1850, the son of a white planter father and an enslaved mother, Mary Ricks.[169] Coming to Texas in 1881, he was deeply committed to improving conditions among black people. Rayner was well known as one of the best speakers in the populist movement, possessing a distinct sense of humor and the Southern gift of storytelling.[170] In 1895, then-Chairman of the People's Party, "Stump" Ashby solicited donations in the *Southern Mercury* to help his fellow committee member Rayner tour the state on behalf of the party, stating, "The work I want Rayner to do no white man can do."[171] Rayner was adept at not only speaking to black audiences about the importance of bringing populism to "picnics, barbecues, encampments, and ordinary mass meetings"; he was also instrumental in founding "colored Populist clubs himself." Preferring to work in rural areas, he was key in spreading the populist message through Texas and challenging the power of the Republican Party with black Texans.[172]

While Rayner was touring the countryside, Melvin Wade was at work with the burgeoning labor movement in Texas towns. By the time populism was in full swing, he had established himself as a Knights of Labor leader and third-party activist. Wade connected the People's Party not only to Texas's black community but also served as an important meeting point between the agrarian revolt and the Texas labor movement, unafraid to use his memories of slavery to stake out a strong position on the abuses of the New South. In 1897, during an Emancipation Day speech held in Dallas, Wade—paraphrased by the *Dallas Morning News*—argued, "The shackles of chattel slavery had been destroyed, but the shackles of industrial slavery had been riveted so tightly that the iron had eaten into the flesh."[173]

But it would take time to earn the trust of black Texans like Melvin Wade. In the founding meeting of the People's Party in Texas, Wade—who had long been a loyal member of the Republican Party—left the meeting after questioning the commitment of the People's Party to confronting unequal treatment of black Texans by the "sheriffs," in the "passenger cars," and on "juries."[174] That meeting, two black men were elected to the first State Executive Committee of the People's Party at its founding in Texas, but Wade would need more convincing.[175] Many—but not all—of the Populists were looking for a way to unite black and white workers. As one white delegate noted, black Texans "are in the ditch just like we are."[176] Ashby warned the delegates at this inaugural meeting:

"[Y]ou are approaching a battlefield in which many errors have been made in the past. The democrats have never given these people representation; they have said they would buy enough of their votes with liquor and money. The republicans have left the negro without a party. If he has a friend it is we, and he can be our friend. If the committee is large, we do not propose to be governed by party regulations in the past. I am in favor of giving the colored men full representation."[177]

With populists leaving the Democrats for the People's Party in droves, and the Lily-white Republicans making clear that they would no longer share the party with black people, the populist movement stood to make major gains, if it played its cards right. Melvin Wade would soon join the movement. Together, farmers and workers, black and white, would force the Democrats' hand. They had to do everything in their power to prevent the rise of populism.

Chapter 8

Educate and Unite The People

Political education was central to Populism. On a practical level, Populists had to be able to push back against the propaganda and daily attacks by newspapermen loyal to their wealthy funders and the Democratic Party. Populists needed papers like the *Southern Mercury* to respond to the muck thrown their way; they also needed supporters willing and educated enough to defend the movement from the constant barrage of attacks from the Democratic press. To do this, Populists created People's Party clubs. The *Southern Mercury* called its readers to organize "populist clubs" to take the reform literature of the party and "scatter it abroad on its mission of converting the people."[178] Winning elections mattered to the party, but there was a broad commitment to long-term political work outside of election season, best embodied in this missive shortly after the 1894 election: "An election has been held, but that is of little consequence. The populist educational campaign goes on regardless of elections."[179]

Populist clubs were meant to be organized on a local scale, with weekly meetings to debate and read populist literature to "educate, elevate and unite the people."[180] Once a month, clubs were to hold all-day meetings to allow members to build relationships with one another. Across Texas, Populist clubs were organized, and members debated strategy, economics, and the coming "cooperative commonwealth." Populists were encouraged to spread the message "not in a patronizing or self-important manner, but in that earnest, unostentatious, patriotic way, that will disarm prejudice, command consideration, and finally secure success."[181] Regular engagement was an opportunity to continue the political work of Populism outside of elections, and produced leaders within the movement. It was seen as critical not just for the electoral success of the Populists, but also for the movement to be successful when it came into power. As the *Southern Mercury* wrote, "The populists realize that governments are but a reflex of the intelligence and morals of the people, and that the only possible hope of purifying the government is to educate the masses."[182]

Encampments, the large festivals and meetings of like-minded populists, continued, as did the lecturing system perfected under the Farmers' Alliance.[183] It is difficult to imagine an equivalent to the Populist encampments today. Attendance was often in the thousands, and even up to fifteen thousand attendees were not beyond expectations.[184] The carnival-like atmosphere was complete with merry-go-rounds, barbecue, and even dancing (though this was "set well to the side" to avoid the ire of the older attendees).[185] The events would last upwards of a week, with speeches and opportunities to meet the famous and influential Pops, and time to enjoy music, prayers, and sermons. As political scientist Roscoe Martin puts it, "For a whole week they lived and breathed reform: by day and by night they sang of Populism, they prayed for Populism, they read Populist literature and discussed Populist principles with their brethren in the faith."[186]

Populism is an abused term today, often narrowly defined as political rhetoric wielding an us-versus-them style. This common usage does a disservice to actually existing populism, which was much more than a rhetorical style. It was a living, breathing movement of people. While Populists certainly had a political slant, the movement took an optimistic view of "the people," even those who had not yet become populists. Populism believed in the common people, not just for who they were but for who they could be. Through engagement and education, populism would not only win politically, they believed, but through that collective struggle, they would also become more complete individuals.

This is the radical promise that populism offered, the belief that it would take work, discipline, and education, but through that, yes, the tenant farmer, the railroad worker, and the baker could govern. The radical democratic promise of populism can be understood by reading its party platforms, its lecturers' great speeches, and through the prose of its best writers. But it is best understood in the enthusiasm of its everyday members—the families camped out, sitting by the fire, debating the political questions of their day. They were not the followers of some leader known as a Populist; they were, as a group, Populists—a movement of people for the people.

Chapter 9

A Strike, An Election, and Fraud

The Panic of 1893 brought the economic depression that had been ravaging the rural South to the cities.[187] People were thrown out of work, and the panic led to bank runs, exacerbating the crisis. It hit the railroad industry hard. The companies that survived responded by squeezing labor, leading to the Pullman Strike of 1894. After the rail company lowered wages, workers organizing in the American Railway Union went on a wildcat strike. The strike turned violent after President Cleveland, in his non-consecutive second term, sent in the U.S. Army to crush it. The brutal violence of the Cleveland administration against the workers and the jailing of labor leader, future Socialist Party presidential candidate Eugene Debs, was not taken lightly. The attack on labor radicalized many Knights of Labor in Texas toward third-party politics, with one Knight boldly asserting his allegiance to populism while condemning Grover Cleveland's government as "one of the most damnable administrations that has ever disgraced the annals of American history."[188]

This sentiment was echoed by none other than Eugene Debs himself, the *Southern Mercury* quoted at length: "My advice to you is to go and vote the populist ticket, and take this misused power from the railroads and put it in the hands of the government."[189] The 1894 election provided a historic opportunity for the People's Party. Black and white lecturers had won trust amongst black voters in the People's Party, and further inroads with laborers and farmers were being made daily. Infighting inside both the Republican and Democratic Party allowed the People's Party to pick up voters from both camps. Last, the Populists were no longer just a rural phenomenon, with the 1894 results showing impressive gains in the urban areas of the state, especially those near railroad depots and with Knights of Labor locals.[190] If William Lamb and "Stump" Ashby's support for labor had laid the foundation for the Knights of Labor to more openly align with the Populists, the brutal actions of the Democrats against labor cemented it.[191]

When the votes were counted in Texas, the Populist Thomas Nugent had received thirty-six percent of the vote in a three-way race, overtaking the Republican Party to become the second-largest in the state. In a few short years, the People's Party had moved from a small coalition of radical elements of the labor movement and Farmers' Alliance into a major player in Texas politics. Further victories seemed certain. But there were signs that Democrats had tampered with election results.

Intimidation of Populists was rampant in 1894. The Democratic Party used its control of state employment to intimidate voters in Texas. In Huntsville, Texas, for instance, penitentiary workers were forced by their state employer to sign a loyalty pledge to the Democratic Party. If they refused, they were fired on the spot.[192] Voting at this time was typically done through a party ballot, where the names of party candidates in each race were listed out. There were reports that election officials, mostly Democrats, conveniently ran out of Populist Party ballots early in the morning on election day.[193] Even worse was the ballot stuffing, intimidation, and fraud in black communities. The Democratic candidate for governor, Charles Culberson, racked up suspiciously high numbers in some counties with a large black population—some, like Harrison County, as high as ninety-four percent, way out of proportion with other parts of the state.[194] The results were equally suspect in the Sixth Congressional District, where Jerome Kearby ran a strong race. Ballot stuffing, throwing out ballots, and early closing of the polls were all alleged by the People's Party.[195] The results of the elections were good for the Populists, but the outright fraud and intimidation of the voters previewed a challenge for Populism. Would Democrats allow them to win, or would they cling to power even if it meant running sham elections? One thing was clear: If Populists hoped to win, they'd need to gain even larger majorities.

Factional fights in both the Republican and Democratic Party provided the Populists a tempting opportunity for improving their position. While Texas Populists had success statewide, only the Western states were able to send Populists to Congress. These states were not under the thumb of the Democratic Party machine and were well represented in the national People's Party. Due to the success of the Populists, the issue of free silver, the unlimited coinage of silver, had found a home in the Democratic Party. Grover Cleveland's disastrous economic policies, his stubborn devotion to the gold standard, created a fissure between Democrats. In the country's South and West, continued opposition to free silver would be politically catastrophic. And by incorporating the silver plank into the Democratic platform, the hope was that this would end the populist revolt, leading Populists to "return unto the house of their fathers."[196] James Hogg, who had risen to power by redirecting agrarian anger to his own purposes before, was even favored by some to become the Democratic Party nominee for the 1896 election. But it was William Jennings Bryan who would receive the Democratic nomination, after successfully outmaneuvering Cleveland supporters and the Eastern wing of the Democratic Party. The Populists had forced the "party of their fathers" to change, but this success would threaten the People's Party's independence.

The People's Party convention was held after the Republican and Democratic Party. This allowed them to react to the factional fights in both organizations. While Texas seemed on the cusp of going Populist, the Populists nationally were at a crossroads. The silver issue had finally gone from being treated as a fringe issue to a fierce debate capable of cleaving through the old parties. How to react? If either of the old parties were to endorse the silver issue, then the Populists could seize the momentum, either by "fusing" with one of the old parties, or through running a separate campaign for a pro-silver candidate called "the middle of the road strategy."[197] Fusing with the Democratic Party was unacceptable to the Texas delegation, who had fought hard to win political independence, but not to other national Populists, who were ready to run a "fusion ticket." Despite the valiant attempts of the Texas delegation, the Populist national convention endorsed William Jennings Bryan and Tom Watson, a populist, for vice president, over the Democrats' conservative choice of Arthur Sewall.

Tom Watson's selection was actually a victory for the "middle of the roaders" who, in spite of their name, represented the more committed radicals of the People's Party. Bryan and the Democrats would either have to submit to the People's Party's demands, or reject their endorsement, leaving open the chance to stake out their independence later on. As voting at the convention was taking place, word came that Bryan wouldn't accept the nomination. But this information, either by accident or by trickery, was not relayed to People's Party delegates until after the vote.

The Texas delegation suspected something was afoot and tried to delay the vote. It seemed that "fusion" was inevitable. Defiantly, the great Texas leader "Stump" Ashby interrupted every roll-call vote of the convention to ask if word had come as to whether Bryan would accept their Party's nomination.[198] After each vote, the chair would not acknowledge that Bryan had refused. Although the Texas chapter was one of the most electorally successful, the People's Party had accepted rules that assigned delegates based on state population, not party strength. This diluted Texas's influence and strengthened states like New York, which had more people but a much weaker party.[199] The final ballot, which pitted "fusion" with the Democrats against maintaining independence, overwhelmingly favored fusion. The vote to endorse William Jennings Bryan and "fuse" with the Democrats went 1,047 to 331.[200] Every single Texas delegate voted to remain independent, leading those 103 to be known as the "immortal 103."

While most Texas populists generally were united on the opposition to fusion, the crisis was rife with opportunism. The respected orator "Cyclone" Davis had come out for fusion and argued passionately that Populists align themselves with the Democratic Party, surprising many. This led chairman "Stump" Ashby to call Davis "an enemy of reform."[201] Davis' enthusiasm for the coming state of affairs was seen as a major betrayal among Texas populists who remained committed to the third-party movement and against compromise with the Democratic Party. In the *Southern Mercury* J.D. Cady wrote that, while he was ashamed of various national Populist leaders for fusing with the Democrats, "My shame, sorrow, mortification and regret is at its zenith when I reach Cyclone Davis." Speaking to the personal and emotional way that "Cyclone" Davis' betrayal was experienced, Cady said,

> "he was a man whom I had learned to love. I hate for Texas to have to give up a man of such talents, but I doubt now that he was ever conscientious, ever hunting for anything except boodle and self-aggrandizement... [he has] thrown us back at least four years, if not longer."[202]

The People's Party went through historic growth in just a few years because it successfully connected urban labor with an increasingly impoverished agricultural movement. As a protest movement, it got the issue of silver to the mainstream of the Democratic Party, but silver was only one of Populism's planks. It was also the least threatening demand to those in power. The stubborn attachment to a gold standard by the U.S. government, despite the instability it caused, provided a compelling argument, and recruitment tool, for the Populist movement and its reforms. It was compelling politically because it exposed just how corrupt and bloated U.S. politics had become: Neither party would even consider the question until an uprising demanded it. But it was because of its simplicity as an issue that the Democrats were able to absorb populism's most popular demand. Contrary to how it was coopted, the Populist critique of the monetary system went deeper than merely which metal was used. What was immediately needed was an expansion of the money supply. Silver was a quick and efficient means toward that end, but the fact that the control of the money supply was determined by artificial scarcity and private power in the first place was the movement's true critique.[203] The silver issue was not populism. It was a part of populism; and, in a way, it was the end of populism, because it led to it becoming so easily absorbed into the Democratic Party.

The Populists were not without other significant achievements. Populist demands, watered down, became incorporated in the reform democrat and the progressive platforms of the coming era. But the insurgency that drove the Populist movement would wane, while the populism of the Democratic Party would become a populism without the people. Some of the Populist leaders would join up with the Democrats; others would continue the fight for the next few years until the People's Party's eventual demise. The Democrats' attitude toward the Populists is best captured by National Democratic Party Chairman Jones's response to People's Party advocates who had asked him to consider Tom Watson as William Jennings Bryan's running mate. He said they should "go with the Negroes, where they belong."[204]

While Populism began to collapse inside of the Democratic Party, in other parts of the country, including Texas, the fight continued. Most histories of populism end with the fusion with William Jennings Bryan, but in Texas, the home of the "immortal 103," populism would not disappear so easily. Thomas Nugent had died in 1895, leading the Populists to select Jerome Kearby to lead the ticket. When the votes were counted in 1896, the People's Party had continued to grow; they lost by just 60,000 votes, with nearly 44 percent of the vote in their favor. But any celebration had been dampened by the events of election day: "Democrats responded with everything from charges of racial treason to bribery, stuffing ballot boxes, and shooting Populist organizers."[205] It is almost certain that the election was rigged to ensure the Democrats won. History is rife with accounts of Populist candidates being attacked in the street by gangs of Democratic Party thugs and other intimidation. One harrowing tale, set in Robertson Valley, where the great black Populist John B. Rayner resided, sets the scene of the 1896 election. After "deposing" the black town marshal, "forty men armed with Winchester rifles then stationed themselves around the courthouse, allowing only Democrats to enter to vote."[206] Across Texas, there were reports of masked men robbing ballot boxes, ballot manipulation, and other trickery, like listing the name of the Democratic candidate, Culberson, on the Populist ballot.[207] The Populists "officially" lost by 60,000 votes, but the result of 1896 is recognized by many "as almost certainly fraudulent."[208] Five Congressional races, too, had suspiciously close margins, but all were narrow defeats for Populism. Maybe "Cyclone" Davis was right: The Populists had to "fuse" with Democrats to win, but only because the Democrats would not allow themselves to be beaten in a free and fair election—and had the full force of the state and mob violence to enforce the rules as they saw fit.

After populism, "Cyclone" Davis eventually more fully embraced the fusionist position. He joined the KKK and, in 1916, was elected to Congress as a Democrat.[209] Writing about Davis' election to Congress, the Socialist paper *The Rebel* memorably ridiculed the former Populist: "THE DOG HATH RETURNED TO HIS VOMIT."[210] William Lamb, the man who in many ways was responsible for Texas Populism and presided over the founding meeting of the Texas People's Party, immediately faced tragedy. Soon after achieving his political goals, Lamb was sued for libel by a Democrat for an ad in his paper, even though Lamb had been away from his press when it was published. A Democratic Party judge found Lamb responsible. The decision ruined him financially and made him all but ineligible to run for office or be publicly associated with the People's Party. This successful attack on the great Populist leader effectively side-lined him from politics, and he was not put up for office despite holding the respect of many Texas radicals, then and today.

While unsuccessful in politics, he formed a successful small-scale version of the "Subtreasury" in Northern Texas, achieving a taste of the collective ideals to which he dedicated his life. In 1906, he won prizes for his revolutionary hybrid fruits, and he stayed radical till the end of his days.[211] The other radicals, S.O. Daws, who brought the Farmers' Alliance to life with a "travelling lecturer" program and the Populist leader and former carnival clown "Stump" Ashby, moved up to Oklahoma and continued the fight.[212] These "Pops," as they were known, cut through Texas's race regime, took on the entrenched political power of the railroads, banks, and Southern Democrats, and never flinched. Their work inspired future generations of Texas radicals in their fight for a better world.

In meetings and town squares over the coming years in Texas and the South, the most radical voice would often come from the back of the crowd, softly but boldly spoken by an old white-haired and whiskered "Pop." Decades later, as the next fight for the common people stirred, "Stump" Ashby was asked if he would once again travel the state. He replied saying he had given "the best years of his life in defense of the people," but "now I am old and poor... I am sorry that I am not younger and in better financial shape."[213] It was time for the next generation of Texans to take on the fight, which had begun with a few radical cowboys and farmers in a humble barn in Lampasas, Texas.

PART 2

Let Us Arise

Chapter 10

From Populism To Socialism

On May 17, 1917, four Texas Rangers surrounded Thomas Hickey—the red-haired, Irish-born leader of the Texas Socialist Party—and made no secret that they were well armed. Led by the one-armed John Montgomery, the Rangers had been waiting for Hickey to head to the post office in Brandenburg, where two forks of the Brazos River meet. "Red Tom" Hickey was especially easy to spot that day, carrying 60 sheets of newspaper copy he'd written for *The Rebel*, the Texas Socialist Party's weekly. Producing no warrant for his arrest and brandishing their guns, the Rangers ordered Hickey into their car.

At the time, it was not unheard of for socialists, radicals, and labor leaders to be disappeared. Hickey was held for days, his telegrams to his wife and comrades suppressed. Eventually, he was charged with helping "draft resistance," which was justification enough for the federal government to shut down *The Rebel*. His captors claimed they had evidence that Tom Hickey had planned an "insurrection against the government," with plans "to seize Abilene, cut all the telephone wires and telegraph wires, dynamite all the railroads, seize the banks and grocery stores, put torch to the city, ... and generally raise the red and black flags of murder, pillage arson and red revolution."[1] These claims were nonsense, but Hickey's arrest amid the nation's first Red Scare would spell the end for the rising Texas Socialist Party.

The Texas SP had taken up the fight for the working class after Texas Populism was defeated. Soon, it would become the third-largest socialist party in the nation. Like the Populists, the Texas SP would even overtake the Republicans as the second-largest party in the state before facing violent repression, rigged elections, bullets, and police batons. Unlike the Populists, who largely advocated for reforms to the capitalist system, the Texas Reds—as students of Karl Marx—were fighting for nothing less than revolution. Eventually, the Texas SP fell victim to the terror and repression of the first Red Scare. But not before founding a Texan working-class tradition.

Meanwhile, the conditions that had brought about populism were only getting worse. In the first decade of the 1900s, compared to the rest of the United States, "in Texas and Oklahoma there were twice as many tenants over the age of fifty-five and three times as many renters over the age of sixty-five."[2] By 1910, as Texas's socialists were ascendant, 52.9 percent of Texas farms were worked by tenant farmers, a more than 10 percent increase from 1890.[3] While the Populists had won some reforms through "fusion" with the Democrats, few other than a score of politicians and wealthier "Pops" actually benefited.

But the Populists' failures were formative. Many Texan socialists came to their beliefs through recognizing the limits to reformism, which had led to Populism's ultimate collapse. As Martin Irons, the legendary union leader of the Great Southwest Strike of 1886, once said, "Populists are juniors; Socialists are seniors.

All Populists are not Socialists for it is impossible for juniors to be seniors, but all Socialists are Populists and more."[4]

In other words, Populism was a necessary first step for the movement, teaching folks the most effective worker organizing techniques, and what it takes to defeat the Democratic Party. Texas Socialists would continue many Populist traditions: organizing large encampments, prioritizing popular education, and employing a flock of traveling speakers. The region's Populist history provided a unique opportunity to mobilize tenant farmers—a rare tactic among Socialist Party chapters, at least, compared to those in the Midwest—but the Texas SP would also make good on Populist radicals' plan to break in with the state's industrial working class. A new form of politics was being born, welding a distinct Texan perspective together with the wisdom of populism and a serious commitment to the fight for what they called the "cooperative commonwealth." As Eugene Debs said of the men and women of Texas: "these are Socialists, real Socialists, and they are ready for action."[5]

* * *

Populism came within striking distance of ending the two-party system in Texas. To fend it off, the Democrats had resorted to ballot stuffing and rigging elections. As the populist revolt began to crumble, Democrats initiated a series of restrictions to reinforce their hold on power, effectively barring Populists from participating in Democratic Party affairs. For the Democrats' left wing, this created a new problem: By liquidating the Populists from their ranks, the party's conservative bloc became the strongest in the room. To fix this, party members turned to former Governor Hogg, who had so capably tied the Farmers' Alliance into knots by offering a slow trickle of reforms. Hogg convinced Democrats to weaken its voter restrictions and, importantly, recommit to railroad and corporate reform.[6] It took multiple election cycles, but by 1902, the more conservative (and whiter) congregations of the agrarian revolt were pulled back into the Democratic fold.

Meanwhile, Democrats also disenfranchised black voters by introducing a poll tax and "White Man's Primaries"—breaking another pillar of the People's Party broad coalition. Workers, black and white, would have to pay between $1.50 and $1.75 to vote. As previously mentioned, many farmers were already perpetually in debt, and most made "little more than $425 a year," meaning most working Texans were effectively disenfranchised in this period.[7] It's not surprising that voting rates in Texas plummeted following these "reforms."[8] In one fell swoop, former Populists only had one ally they could turn to—the Hogg wing of the Democratic Party—or else Democrats' conservative faction would reign supreme. Many Populist leaders went along with the changes, embracing the tradeoff for influence. Notably, as historian Thomas Alter II notes in his rich account of the German roots in Texas's radical history, German Texans who had been so central to Texas radicalism up to this point took the opportunity provided in the new primary system to "enter the white mainstream."[9] Though many in leadership took this deal, a fair amount of former Populist voters rejected it. The 1902 election—the year the poll tax was officially adopted—saw the "largest opposition to disenfranchisement centered in North Texas," a hotbed of Populism. This was no sure thing—many

Populist leaders actually *supported* the poll tax, but among the People's Party rank and file, "Eighty-one percent of those voting the Populist ticket in 1902 opposed the poll tax."[10]

Concurrent with Democrats' disenfranchisement campaign, many whites took to the streets to enact terror. For example, in Grimes County, once a Populist stronghold, "a white Populist sheriff and his black deputy" were targeted by "vigilante Democrats."[11]

The Sheriff, Garrett Scott, had held his position for years, working closely with his friend and ally Jim Kennard, a black man elected District Clerk in 1882.[12] Together with Jack Haynes and Morris Carrington, also black, who left Republican Party politics for the People's Party, the four appeared to offer an alternative vision for small-town Texas governance. It was bad enough for Grimes County white supremacists that blacks and whites were fraternizing, but the fact they were winning elections was flat out unacceptable. There was little they could publicly do at the time—Populism was extremely popular in the region, across racial lines—so the town's business elite and the white supremacists organized a White Man's Union in secret. Then, as the People's Party faltered, the White Man's Union struck.

First, the group published its bylaws in the local paper, inviting white men to put aside their differences: "What a grand picture ... democrats and populists after all these years of strife and bitter wrangling ... stepping out on the high plain of true American manhood." To their black neighbors—who made up nearly half of Grimes County's population—the WMU claimed, "the Southern white man is still his best friend .... But we shall insist that the white man is the most competent one to hold the offices."[13] Soon, the Union was menacingly visiting the homes of known white populists, and under the threat of violence, black men in town were intimidated from voting in local elections.

Garrett Scott urged the white populists to arm themselves in defense of their black neighbors. Some may have heeded Scott's warning, but it wasn't enough. The first to be killed in the terror was Jim Kennard, shot within shouting distance of the courthouse.[14] No one was brave enough to testify, but most knew the killer to be J.G. McDonald, who had founded the White Man's Union after losing the county judge seat in 1898. Then the state government stepped in—on behalf of the WMU. Against loud protestations from Sheriff Garrett Scott and the People's Party, Texas Adjutant General Thomas Scurry permitted the local Texas State Guard to march in a parade organized by the WMU.[15] This show of force, and Scott's inability to stop it, foretold what was coming. Jack Haynes was killed, shot with a shotgun on his own cotton farm.[16]

Black people began fleeing the county en masse, voter turnout dropped over 50%, and People's Party candidates began withdrawing their names from the ballot.[17] But Garrett Scott wasn't one to back down. He defiantly told a WMU leader to "go and get your Union force, every damn one of them, put them behind rock fences and trees and I'll fight the whole damn set of cowards."[18]

Scott lost his reelection campaign, but the WMU wasn't done with him. Days after the election, Scott's residence above the jail was surrounded. Scott's family members, hearing word of the WMU attack, rushed to town to help him. Scott's brother was killed, but not before returning fire and sending his killer to justice. Meanwhile, Scott was gravely wounded; his sister dragged him into the jailhouse to escape the WMU. For the next five days, Scott holed up in the jailhouse and exchanged gunfire with WMU goons. At his side were his deputies, black and white. On the fifth day, an escort of Texas State Guards arrived to escort Garrett Scott out of Grimes County.[19] This is how populism—and a multiracial version of governance— was defeated in Grimes County. Political and economic elites fomented a vengeful white supremacy to choke off populism's promise, and one-party rule returned to Texas.

Given the scope of the violence, it may be surprising that social-ism was able to take root in the state during this time at all. But the Texas socialists were committed. As one West Texas tenant farmer wrote, "we must work together to help our brethren see the light. Give us Socialism and the religion of our Lord and Savior Jesus Christ."[20]

Chapter 11

The Early Socialists

William E. Farmer was among the first to buck the People's Party. In 1898, he formed the Texas Social Democratic Party in Bonham, a small town around 70 miles north of Dallas. He and his compatriots intended to pursue Texas independence and create a socialist republic in the Lone Star State, but the great railway union leader Eugene Debs talked them out of that. Instead, Debs encouraged them to merge with the Social Democratic Party of America.[21] Many radicals had wanted Debs to lead the People's Party in the fateful 1896 convention, but he declined. Now, he was dedicated to rekindling an independent working-class politics in the United States.

Debs had long been an important labor leader, but he was not always the godfather of American socialism. At times, he had even sided with the union bureaucracy against the rank-and-file. For instance, during the Great Southwest Strike of 1886—recounted in Chapter 5—Debs had joined other national labor leaders in refusing to support the Knights of Labor and Martin Irons in their effort to take on Jay Gould's railway.[22] Gould and the U.S. government used brutal force to put down the 1886 strike, after which the Knights of Labor began losing membership, and thus waned in power nationally. For a time, though, in

Texas, the Knights lived on, due to their close-knit relationship with the Populists. Once the People's Party fell, the Knights disappeared along with them.[23]

Debs fully broke with the labor establishment around the 1894 Pullman Strike, which shut down U.S. freight and passenger traffic west of Detroit, and ended after the federal government swooped in, sentencing Debs to six months in prison. By the time he reconnected with William Farmer and Martin Irons, he was a committed revolutionary. The great labor leader Martin Irons is buried near Waco, Texas, a humble monument to a giant of the Texas labor movement. Although he would not live long into the socialist movement, he was an indispensable link between 19th- and 20th-century radicalism. Eugene Debs described Irons, whose labor radicalism was a personal inspiration to him, as a man who "bore the traces of poverty and broken health," but when "he spoke of socialism, he seemed transformed and all the smouldering fires within him blazed once more from his sunken eyes."[24]

The fiery, bloody struggles in Texas, the Midwest, and the South that produced Debs and Irons were not the only cauldrons of American socialism at the time. In New York City, the Marxist Daniel De Leon, spent the 1890s in the Socialist Labor Party. In the previous decade, De Leon had even practiced law in Brownsville, Texas, a stone's throw from Mexico, but soon he returned to New York—the city being much more to his liking. De Leon instructed a generation of socialists, among them, the Irish-born "Red Tom" Hickey, later heralded as the "uncrowned king of Texas socialism."[25] In the decades to come,

Hickey would join Eugene Debs in the Socialist Party, but in the 1890s Hickey held a special contempt for Debs' followers, labelling his followers "Debsomanics."[26] De Leon and his followers felt that Debs, who had only recently converted to socialism after the 1894 Pullman Strike, represented an unsophisticated strain of the political movement. Debs' lack of study and conversion through personal experience was seen as a weakness, and De Leon's acolytes warned that Debs would lead his followers back into reformism and away from revolutionary politics. Texas socialists like William Farmer were fierce critics of the American Marxist Daniel De Leon, who they called a "Grand inquisitor" with a "military" form of political organization.[27] Soon Tom Hickey would learn just how correct the critics were. He was among the many purged from De Leon's Socialist Labor Party by a vindictive and angry De Leon who blamed everyone but himself for its failures.[28]

The "agrarian question" has always been difficult for Marxist theorists, especially in the United States: Even though it had industrial centers in the 20th century, much of its economy was thoroughly agricultural. Even in America, Marxist thinkers misunderstood agrarian labor in the South. Often, farmers were labelled "petty bourgeois," or even "bourgeois," because they owned the land and therefore would be opposed to common ownership or collectivization—a fancy way of saying the economic interests of farmers made them opposed to collective ownership of the means of production. But this perspective was mistaken, especially when it came to the South. The history of slavery and the fact that land was concentrated in the hands of large landholders and financial interests created a dynamic much different from the Midwest and the Northeast.[29] The "Pope of Marxism" himself, Karl Kautsky, severely misread this situation, writing in 1902 that Southern farmers "are the people from which we have least of all to expect," adding:

> "They may be ripe for a revolt of desperation, and when the proletariat will seize the political power in the industrial districts, the oppressed farmers in the South will not oppose them and will help in their own way. But it seems to me impossible to found a permanent party organization with them."[30]

Kautsky was no fool; many American socialists also failed to recognize the revolutionary potential of tenant farmers, believing that only populism, not socialism, would ever appeal to Southern farmers. In reality, Texas and Oklahoma would lead the nation in producing socialists.

While some had held up their noses at the possibility of a socialist agrarian revolt, Julius Wayland and his newspaper *The Appeal To Reason* was busy at work converting Populists into socialists. Wayland had converted from populism to socialism in the 1890s and dedicated his life to encouraging others to do the same. His paper's base of operations moved around before settling in Girard, Kansas. Self-education and socialist papers were integral to the movement's success, but no paper could rival *The Appeal's* success in making socialists. In 1907, *The Appeal* had a circulation of over 300,000, with a large concentration in Texas and Oklahoma. Not only was it an essential tool in converting farmers into socialists, but because it had such a broad reach, it also helped organize these rural members and connect rural farmers with the wider socialist movement.[31] One issue of *The Appeal* printed a million issues, and nearly the entire town of Girard was enlisted in helping Wayland mail the papers across the country.[32]

Early on, hardline critics complained that *The Appeal* was not rigorous enough and too plain spoken and intellectually vague in its condemnation of capitalism. The paper printed a scathing response to these critiques:

> If the people were Socialists, there would be no need for the Appeal. Its mission is to interest those who are NOT Socialists, in economic problems. It has doubtless interested more people in the subject than all the other publications combined."[33]

This fact is undeniable. Many socialists cited Wayland's *Appeal* as the reason for their conversion.[34] Today, political education is too often dismissed by activists who claim working people don't "have the time, interest, or capacity" to engage in the complex questions. That perspective is as wrong today as it was then. While illiteracy was higher in Texas than in other parts of the country, that did not stop would-be socialists from engaging in socialist education. Traditions of "readings on the porch or before the fireplace was quite common in rural America."[35] For those curious enough to investigate, the socialist press offered plenty of engaging and timely answers to pressing questions. Political education is not just about having the right answers, but building a communal understanding of the world, history, and politics. What are our front-porch readings today? Farmers taught themselves history and politics, as did Southern prisoners at the time, who were "known to teach themselves to read and to master whole disciplines."[36] And as the historian James R. Green noted, "the rural poor of the Southwest, who were also very isolated, searched in a remarkably determined way for information that would explain their desperate condition and lead them to liberation."[37]

Publications like *The Appeal To Reason* were joined, in 1911, by the Texas paper *The Rebel*, published by Thomas Hickey and E.O. Meitzen in Hallettsville, the midway point between San Antonio and Houston. In its inaugural issue, Thomas Hickey made no small promise for the future: "With the complete overthrow of the present anarchistic, war breeding, cannibalistic, women killing cradle robbing system of capitalism civilization will be developed and humanity shall step on to a higher plane."[38] While *The Rebel* and other socialist papers did not self-censor on capitalism and revolution, much like the populist papers of the 1890s, they framed this politics as a continuation of the American revolutionary tradition. Hickey's fiery introduction to the paper ends with a quotation from none other than Benjamin Franklin: "Private property is the creature of society and as such is subject to the demands of society down to the last farthing."[39]

Among the most important organizing tools Texas Socialists turned to were the festival-like encampments they inherited from the Populist movement, but tweaked them for their times. Instead of hearing of the glory of the Subtreasury plan, socialists would attend gatherings in the thousands—some even larger in Oklahoma—sometimes at the height of the Texas summer, to learn about socialism. How to throw a successful encampment? Richey Alexander, an insurance salesman and socialist, was an expert in these matters. Success was contingent on booking the very best speakers. Socialism had many who had perfected the craft, learning from the best of the populist tradition; a good speaker would ensure success. Speeches from the likes of Eugene Debs, Mother Jones, Thomas Hickey, E.O. Meitzen, Kate O'Hare, and others drew thousands of farmer radicals to the encampments.[40]

These were more than just speaking tours. Successful encampments would attract families who would pitch their tents for up to a week, potentially longer, and they needed more than just lectures. Securing "concessions to keep the kids happy," and barbecue, which has always brought Texans together, and these gatherings were no different.[41] Music, dancing, and other attractions would be needed, but planning was necessary. It was critical for attractions like the "concession stand or merry go round" not to "be too near the speakers."[42] A brass band, while nice, should only be hired if "you have money to waste."[43] To give a sense of how these encampments were advertised, a flyer reprinted in James Green's *Grassroots Socialism* for The Mammoth Tenth Annual Socialist Encampment boasted "three addresses daily" by speakers who will "prove Socialism will give every man an equal opportunity to labor, with hand or brain, and receive the full product of his toil undiminished by legalized robbery." The grounds in Grand Saline, east of Dallas, promised "pure, limpid water," as well as plenty of "dense shade," a "ferris wheel," and "all kinds of attractions that make an enjoyable and festive occasion."[44]

Eugene Debs couldn't help but describe these meetings ecstatically. Recalling his tour across Texas and Oklahoma, he wrote of the farmers and families he saw: "they look you straight in the eye with an expression of comradeship so honest and guileless that one cannot resist putting his arms about them... these farmers have the true socialist spirit."[45] Debs had traveled and spoken in many places at many events, but he was profoundly moved by a Texas encampment. He saw his faith in the prospect of a better future revived, ending his report, "Humanity cannot go backward and downward to the caves and the jungles, but most go onward and upward toward God and the light."[46]

Chapter 12

Give Us Socialism And Our Lord And Savior Jesus Christ

The Reverend G.G. Hamilton, a Methodist from Cromwell, Texas, once participated in "several heated debates" in Oklahoma with the Socialist Stanley Clark. He saw socialism as an affront to the individual relationship between a person and Jesus Christ, objected to the "free love" he claimed socialists promoted, and treated the collectivism of socialism as antithetical to his religion. But in these debates, something miraculous happened: the Reverend changed his mind. Stanley Clark suggested that Hamilton read *Christianity and the Social Crisis* by Baptist minister Walter Rauschenbusch—a text that called on the church to fight for economic and social justice, which would later influence Martin Luther King Jr.—and the Texas minister obliged. Shortly after, in dramatic fashion, Reverend Hamilton, "the hardest and most persistent fighter of Socialism in the State of Texas," declared himself a Socialist.[47]

"Society suffers a social disease," Hamilton said in his conversion speech which *The Rebel* proudly published. "The present system of production and exchange puts the greed of one set of men against the humanity of another set of men; it puts dividends above human lives."[48] Although he would lose his Methodist ministry over his proclamation, his statement was a major public victory for these Texas socialists, and he eventually found a new home as a lecturer in the Church of Christ.[49] "Comrade Hamilton" suddenly had plenty of praise for Karl Marx. According to this Texas minister, the Father of Socialism "was able to prophesy just the things are today taking place before our eyes."[50] To think, the man who once feared free love and collectivism ended his powerful conversion speech by saying, "I believe that Socialism is fundamentally right, and I believe in the honesty and good sense of the masses... I had rather trust the masses than the masters."[51]

Just as Populists blended American iconography with the Biblical in their speeches, so too did Christianity profoundly influence American socialism. Most of the religious members of the Socialist Party were "not formally attached to any form of organized religion," but were still compelled by a Christian worldview.[52] While *The Rebel*'s position was to "treat religion as a private affair and request sensation-seeking preachers to keep their hands off," the paper also published a popular "Five Minute Sermon" column. The religious language of Texas socialism—similar as it is to that of the populists—has led some to misread the movement as a more radical outgrowth of populism. And indeed, next to European socialist writing of the time, the religious cadence of Texas socialism might look out of place. This can be seen throughout the writings of many Socialists, like Thomas Hickey, who often employed language indistinguishable from a sermon. Certainly, letters like this one from a Texas railroad worker published in *The Rebel* stand out:

"Capitalism has been weighed in the balance and found wanting. As sure as God reigns, Babylon is falling to rise no more. The international socialist commonwealth—God's Kingdom—shall rise on the wreck and ruin of the world's present ruling powers."[53]

For many Texas socialists, the connection between their religion and a socialist future was certain. It would be a mistake to see this as the movement going light on Marx. Socialists regularly called upon one another to read Marx and other important figures of political economy, but they did so without muddying their message with jargon. Christian metaphor allowed figures like Hickey to relate to Texans with a common political language, without watering down the political or economic analysis. Capitalism was an affront to Christianity, as Marx himself wrote in the *Communist Manifesto*: "The bourgeoisie has stripped of its halo every occupation hitherto honoured and looked up to with reverent awe. It has converted the physician, the lawyer, the priest, ... into its paid wage labourers."[54]

But Religious language served another purpose: warding off the charges of godlessness and "free-love" that Hamilton's old allies—right-wing preachers, Democrats, and business-aligned newspapermen—still bandied about, aiming to dissuade "good Christians" from being pulled astray. But wresting religion away from conservative fanatics would never be enough to spread socialism. If Texas socialists found themselves somewhere between Karl Marx and Jesus, they understood that—to win— they needed more than just ideas. They needed an organized working class. As a 1916 edition of *The Rebel* said, "'Force is the midwife of all Social Revolutions,' said Karl Marx. History says the same thing. Therefore, ORGANIZE GET POWER!"[55]

Chapter 13

The Texas Program

The Texas SP began seeing its greatest electoral successes in the 1910s. Its 1910 platform, adopted in Corpus Christi, called for the abolition of the poll tax, the end of child labor, and the "full right of franchise to women."[56] The Texas Socialist Party had long affirmed women's suffrage; for example, the first southern woman to run for Congress—in 1906, fourteen years before the ratification of the 19th Amendment—was the Texan socialist schoolteacher, Laura Payne.[57] Economically, it called for an eight-hour workday, an "extension of the State Railway" employing workers at union rates, and the "state ownership of cotton gins, cotton seed oils mills... and other utilities in their nature public."[58] There were provisions for a healthcare system with doctors and surgeons employed by the state in each county, along with state-run pharmacies.[59] On the land question, the Texas Reds aimed for the state to purchase the land of "non-resident land owners," implement a "graduated land tax on all farmland held for exploitation or speculation," and to limit the tax on landless farmers' tools.[60]

When compared to contemporary socialist demands, it is notable that the Texas SP, along with the national party, was much more vocal about the importance of social ownership of the means of production and production itself, compared to the more redistributionist focus of the two Bernie Sanders presidential campaigns. Whereas today many democratic socialists demand increased state services funded by tax increases on the rich, the Texas Socialist Party argued that the inequality and capitalist exploitation of workers and farmers could "be changed only by making the ownership of the land and the machinery collective—that is, by making society the owner, instead of the individual."[61]

For the 1910 gubernatorial elections, the Texas SP selected Reddin Andrews, a Confederate veteran and former president of Baylor University. The native Texan always wore a Stetson hat and brought a needed air of respectability to the Texas socialists,[62] but he was no conservative choice. Andrews spoke passionately about socialism as the only way to prevent the coming violence of the 20th century. "Our time is ripe for the pending revolution," he once said. Socialism was the only choice to prevent the coming chaos caused by capitalist inequality, which would lead the world to be "deluged with human blood." Therefore, socialists would use "ballots, not bullets," to effect a "righteous revolution in the interest of the masses."[63,64]

Andrews campaigned across the state and, along with seventeen organizers, made the case that a revolutionary change was needed, especially in rural Texas.[65] Summer encampments featured Big Bill Haywood (founding member and leader of the Industrial Workers of the World), Tom Hickey, Reddin Andrews, and even an editor of *The Appeal,* Fred Warren.[66] When the votes were counted, 11,538 Texans voted socialist in

1910, a growth of thirty percent from the previous election.[67] While the Democrats handily won reelection, the inspiring growth gave Texas Reds rightful confidence that they were emerging as a force to be reckoned with in Texas. The party's 1912 platform reaffirmed its commitment to its 1910 planks, proclaiming, "society is divided into warring groups, based on material interest."[68]

The Rebel launched in 1911, largely in response to the success of the 1910 election, "to teach workers to build a political organization that will seize the political power."[69] The paper vocally supported labor struggles and covered the goings on in renters' unions, but it importantly acted as a megaphone during Eugene Debs' first presidential campaign.

That year, Debs' campaign made two stops in Texas, one in San Antonio and another in Houston. Speaking in front of a packed crowd in Houston, Eugene Debs proclaimed:

> "We have the richest nation in the world; a land exceptionally blessed by nature with a superabundance of natural wealth and yet today there are 10,000,000 of people in this country who were virtually paupers, there were 40,000,000 of people struggling against a poverty that almost overwhelmed them."[70]

Not only was inequality on the rise, but the government was also unresponsive to the people. Debs asked, "Have you ever noticed the other three parties are financed and the personnel of the financiers? They are all backed by the trust heads and Big Business."[71]

The Houston crowd could appreciate the message. In the past, Texas Democrats had responded to the agrarian revolts by making themselves appear more progressive, or picking up ideas from the farmers, like former Governor Hogg had done in the 1890s. But in the 1912 election, with government forces increasingly embarking to snuff out labor activity, Gov. Oscar B Colquitt aligned himself with "conservatives like Senator Joseph Weldon Bailey and lumber 'baron' John Henry Kirby."[72]

As it happens, Debs won 8.5 percent of the Texas vote that year, with a decent number emanating from the "strike-torn piney-woods counties of the East Texas Sabine region."[73] Yet, in the "fiefdoms" of J.H. Kirby, where the lumber baron exerted unchecked power, unlike those other areas around the Sabine, the vote count was markedly suppressed.[74] Meanwhile, Reddin Andrews's second gubernatorial run saw his vote share double to 25,258. While he still lost by a wide margin against the Democratic Party machine, yet again Texas radicals had overtaken the Republican Party as Democrats' main opposition.[75]

* * *

While the Socialist totals might not appear as impressive stacked against the 200,000-plus votes cast for Colquitt, the fact that Socialists polled well at all is remarkable given the scale of disenfranchisement, voter-suppression, and outright rigging at the time in Texas politics. Poll tax payments were due nine months before election day, "at a time when farmers' loans were due and political interest was at a low ebb."[76] Residency requirements meant that many tenants and migrant workers were all but disenfranchised. By 1908, voter turnout in Texas had gone from sixty-one percent in the previous decade to thirty-three percent.[77] In fact, "participation in Texas elections was reduced to one in every seventeen qualified male voters."[78] The ruling class of Texas did not want a repeat of the agrarian revolts of the 1890s. Nothing served this purpose better than stirring up racial resentment. Given the wide array of mechanisms—state violence, union-busting private police forces, racist demagoguery, and more—the relative success of the SP is a testament to just how effective its organizing strategies were, and how hungry the working class was for change.

A key advantage of the Texas SP was the so-called Texas Program, which gave county level chapters significant authority over local affairs, empowered the rank-and-file membership to be decision makers, and created a decentralized form of organization. Only county and state-level secretaries had executive power, and they had to answer to the rank-and-file rather than to a multitude of committees.[79] In a far-flung state like Texas, this provided local chapters with tremendous flexibility. Additionally, it allowed Texas socialists to pursue their own heterodox platform planks from the national party, building off the populist history in Texas.[80] Central among these were the various planks aimed at Texas farmers, especially tenant farmers.

The success of the Texas Program also explains the affinity in Texas for figures like Big Bill Haywood and the Industrial Workers of the World, or IWW, a radical syndicalist labor organization. The Brotherhood of Timber Workers, which operated between Texas and Louisiana, had vast support amongst Texas socialists, unlike the Louisiana SP. This in large part because in Texas the SP was run by a leadership more favorable to the militant and bottom-up form of organizing practiced by the IWW (More to come on the Brotherhood in Chapter 15).

In 1912, the SP removed Big Bill Haywood from the National Executive Committee, in a proposal brought forward by the New York SP and supported by more conservative factions within the party, over accusations that Haywood supported "sabotage."[81] The Texas SP stood with Haywood, and even after his expulsion the IWW were supported by much of the "Red" leadership in the Texas SP.

Chapter 14

Texas Socialism Caught In The Muck

"White tenants are a worthless, lazy, lying anarchist lot. I have kicked every one of them off my farm except one and replaced them with negro laborers, who I can boss and will do what I tell them. My experience with white tenants was disastrous."[82]

This claim from a Texas landlord was emblematic of the way that landlords pitted poor whites and blacks against one another. It was effective. As one white tenant farmer wrote to *The Rebel*, "The land lords have gotten hard on us…We have got to work so much ground and pay rent on it the first year and if we refuse to do that they won't rent to us." The farmer added, "The negro is ruining our country here. They tell us if we don't do like they say that they will rent to negroes."[83] This letter identifies just how landlords were able to use racial divisions to enforce harsh conditions on both white and black tenants.

There were plenty in the Socialist Party advocating a different direction. Eugene Debs himself said, "We are the party of the working class, the whole working class, and we will not suffer ourselves to be divided by any specious appeal to race prejudice; and if we should be coaxed or driven from the straight road we will be lost in the wilderness and ought to perish there."[84] Unfortunately, many Texas socialists got lost in the wilderness.

Especially in its early days, the Texas SP did not do enough to challenge the white supremacist regime of the time, despite calls from party leaders like Eugene Debs. That they were more progressive than many of their contemporaries meant little, when in fact they often reinforced segregation as the norm. For example, in Lavaca County, socialists "abided by Jim Crow norms at its public meetings."[85]

The Texas SP did not reach out to black voters in the same way that the Populists had just a few years prior. Because Democrats had made black participation in civic life all but illegal, one could argue there was little electoral incentive, for a small party with finite resources, to challenge white supremacy. Another argument was that by solely organizing the white working class, the Texas SP might avoid the worst of a state-led crackdown on their party. The conflict they were trying to avoid was inevitable. Had they earned the trust of black Texans beforehand, it might've turned out differently. Meanwhile, state-sanctioned anti-black violence had, for many, obliterated hope that a better world was possible. One white organizer with the SP-aligned Land Renters' Union noted that the movement appealed to black people, but they "were afraid to talk Socialism ... for fear the White Dems would mob them."[86] The decades of racial terror had done its job.

Earlier, I wrote that Texas socialism's Christianity helped ward off charges of "godlessness" or practicing "free love." In the same way, the Democrat-aligned press often accused socialists of favoring racial integration. Unfortunately, Tom Hickey and E.O. Meitzen often took the bait.[87] In one episode outlined by James R. Green, Hickey attempted to flip the script on his Democrat critics who had accused socialists of promoting race mixing by claiming if anyone was actually guilty of race mixing it was the Democrats who, in defense of capitalism, deflated the conditions of white workers and forced them to work side by side with black workers. In doing so, Hickey said, Democrats were creating a "crude 'social equality that would not be possible under Socialism."

The Rebel is rife with articles such as these, routinely appealing to white readers along racial lines. At the same time, The Land Renters' Union, which Hickey helped found in 1911 to assemble tenant farmers, was specifically organized for white tenants. Where some of its aims were truly radical—challenging landlords' power and land ownership as a speculative asset, arguing that "use and occupancy" was the only justifiable claim on land[88]—it also gratingly pitched itself directly to "Mr. White Renter."[89] The Renters' Union was not explicitly socialist, but it was seen as a recruiting tool for bringing tenants into the Socialist Party and drawing a line between renters and landlords. Unlike their neighbors in Oklahoma, who organized their union interracially, the Texas chapter reacted to the fact that white farmers were falling into debt and tenant farming at a faster rate than non-white farmers as a justification for their racialized organizing.[90]

This "bitter race hatred has been a nightmare to every clearseeing socialist working man in the South,"[91] said Oscar

Ameringer, the great Oklahoma socialist. One could imagine a Texas Socialist at the time arguing that the regressive racial policy of the Renters' Union served the purpose of not alienating potential members. But the maintenance of white racial solidarity between landlord and renter only served to reunite the white tenant farmer and landlord arm in arm against black tenants. This limited their membership, and their effectiveness. With tenant farmers divided by race, it was easier for Texas landlords to play one group against another.

In a famous 1903 appeal to anti-racism in the socialist movement, Eugene Debs recalled an encounter with a group of shabbily dressed poor whites at a train depot in Yoakum, Texas, who implored Debs to wait for a "nigger" to carry his bags, because, "That's what he's here for." The four-time socialist presidential candidate noted these men were "themselves the foul product of the capitalist system and held in lowest contempt by the master class, yet esteeming themselves immeasurably above the cleanest, most intelligent and self-respecting Negro, having by reflex absorbed the 'nigger' hatred of their masters." Lambasting the horrors of slavery in the United States, Debs argued, "The whole world is under obligation to the Negro, and that the white heel is still upon the black neck is simply proof that the world is not yet civilized." Socialists in particular owed black people solidarity, "Socialists should with pride proclaim their sympathy with and fealty to the black race, and if any there be who hesitate to avow themselves in the face of ignorant and unreasoning prejudice, they lack the true spirit of the slavery-destroying revolutionary movement."[92] Eugene Debs would regularly appeal to racial solidarity, which the Texas leadership largely ignored. Like the

Populists before them, the Socialists entered that "battlefield in which many errors have been made in the past," and they fell short.[93]

However, the rise of the Brotherhood of Timber Workers in Louisiana and East Texas—in which black and white people found themselves on the same side of the labor struggle from 1910 to 1916—reoriented the Socialist movement. The union of black and white timber workers struck fear into the hearts of the timber barons and reinvigorated the hopes of the multi-racial working-class movement. Socialists were rightfully horrified by the repression the union members faced at the hands of the capitalist class. It also provided a perfect opportunity to expose the stupidity of those "socialists" who still upheld the backward race regime. In *The Rebel*, the poet and Southern revolutionary Covington Hall lambasted the "muttonhead" "white Lumberjacks" and "farmers" who wouldn't join the BTW because it "admitted colored MEN" to the union. "If race lines don't trouble 'em [the ruling class]. Why should they split and defeat labor? Why? We are fools to fall for it."[94]

Chapter 15

The Brotherhood Of Timber Workers

A rich man does not build his own town out of charity and love for democracy; he builds it for control. Company towns, as they were known, have a long history in Texas. Likely the most famous example is Sugar Land, Texas, southwest of Houston, which was controlled by the Imperial Sugar Company and for years relied on slave, and then convict, labor. Nestled deep in the Piney Woods on the border of Louisiana stands Kirbyville, another important company town with a similarly sordid history. At one point, it was controlled entirely by the "Prince of the Pines," timber baron John Henry Kirby.

Kirby ran a feudal-like operation, controlling nearly every aspect of his workers' lives. It was also some of the most dangerous work in the country. Kirby had a paternalistic view of his workforce, and often grandstanded about his "generosity," saying, "every dollar my company has earned has been distributed in wages to my pals."[95] Fancying himself a progressive, Kirby applauded himself for limiting his workers' workdays to *just* ten grueling hours, at an average wage of $1.50 to $2.50 per week. Also, those wages weren't typically paid in dollars; instead, at Kirby's lumber mills, "over 90 per cent" of workers' earnings came in the form of company "scrip wages"—fake money only accepted in the company store.[96] Kirby's so-called "pals," understanding the truth of their position, referred to him facetiously as the "Peon's Pal."[97] These conditions weren't only found in Kirbyville. When black and white workers across Louisiana and East Texas began to organize one of the nation's first interracial unions, they came up against many men like Kirby, who owned many a company town. These timber barons were determined to protect their profits, and they did so by stoking the white supremacist status quo. In 1912, one worker described the conditions people faced in the company towns like this:

> He is born in a Company house; wrapped in Company swaddling clothes, rocked in a Company cradle. At sixteen he goes to work in the Company mill. At twenty-one he gets married in a Company Church. At forty, he sickens with Company malaria, lies down on a Company bed, is attended by a Company doctor who doses him with Company drugs, and then he loses his last Company breath, while the undertaker is paid by the widow in Company scrip for the Company coffin in which he is buried on Company ground.[98]

The timber barons of Louisiana and Texas were born out of abuse of government programs. Following the Civil War, Northern and British syndicates "abused the Homestead Act," buying up land across the cash-poor South "for as little as $1.25 an acre"[99] and receiving a massive return on their investment: "railroads and other northern capitalists [sic] monopolized the market and made enormous profits."[100] John Kirby liked to play a farm boy from East Texas, but he rose to prominence and wealth with the help of a collection of Boston investors.[101] In just twenty years, these syndicates cut so much timber, a U.S. government expert called it "probably the most rapid and reckless destruction of forests known to history."[102]

The work was hard. The Southern lumber industry was among the most hazardous in the country. Roughly 30 percent of the laborers worked in the forest as lumberjacks, where injuries ranged from cuts to the ever-present danger of being crushed by a felled tree. For the other 70 percent of workers in the sawmills, the dangers were plentiful. Men died falling off logs and landing in the band saw, or having their overalls caught on wood as it was being shoved into the grinder, pulling them headfirst to be chopped into mulch.[103] At the same time, bosses were constantly trying to increase the rate of production, going so far as to promote narcotics among their workers. As Big Bill Haywood noted after touring the region, "At every company store, cocaine, morphine, and heroin are sold."[104] When injuries or deaths occurred, the companies would blame workers for their alleged carelessness.

The timber workers themselves were white, black, and Mexican, and the vast majority were Southerners. Unlike lumber operations in other parts of the country, the presence of very few foreigners, along with the large percentage of black workers, gave the Southern industry a unique regional character.[105] Much like the Fence Cutters or the striking cowboys, these workers resisted the regimented form of shift-work and wage labor put into place by their bosses. As the forests were chopped down, displacing the "forest people," they went to work at the lumber mills and brought with them their own traditions. Some returned to their family farm to pick cotton, or refused to work before sunrise, after sunset, or after a long night out on Sunday drinking and doing cocaine; they also refused to work hungover, on what was called "blue Monday."[106] To discipline these workers, the companies hired the sheriffs to get them in line, cracking down on "vice," "bawdy houses," and union organizers.[107] The feudal control, brutal living conditions, and police brutality had to end. But every time the timber workers tried to organize themselves, it ended in failure. That is, until December 1910.[108]

In the words of timber baron John Kirby, Arthur Lee Emerson was a "tin-horn gambler and sawmill loafer... who is a rank socialist and of some attainments as a scholar."[109] Meanwhile, his comrade Jay Smith was "a desperate kind of fellow with a great deal of natural ability but little education," and, Kirby added, "He, too, is a socialist and is by nature a criminal."[110] Both Smith and Emerson were Southern-born. Emerson had spent some time working in the West. When he was working on the Pacific Coast and came across the "Lumber Workers' Union of St. Regis and ... the Bitter Root Range of Mountains," Emerson saw the differences in wages and conditions that could be won in a union.[111] He committed himself to a labor revolution, moved back South, and worked out a way to organize an interracial union.[112] By December 3, 1910 Emerson organized his first chapter of the Brotherhood of Timber Workers (BTW), in Carson, Louisiana.[113] The union was committed to organizing both black and white workers into "one big union," and for this, it met stiff resistance.[114] In its constitution, the union demanded "Recognition, Equal Rights, A Living Wage, A just consideration of abuses." They even offered a fig leaf to Kirby and the employers—"an absolutely square deal"—promising that the workers were interested in meeting and hearing out the position and needs of their employer.[115] The thought of workers being able to make their own demands—let alone being forced to actually cede to them—infuriated Kirby, who immediately began surveilling and plotting the BTW's downfall.

John Kirby had already helped organize a Southern Lumber Operators' Association, an organization primarily set up to defeat organized labor in the timber industry.[116] To keep the BTW out, the SLOA used "yellow dog" contracts, which explicitly forbade employees from joining a union, and kept a blacklist of workers fired elsewhere for union organizing.[117] To counter this, the BTW practiced secrecy, leaning on "the usual passwords and grips so dear to Southerners, regardless of race," said the socialist ally of the BTW, Covington Hall.[118] The bosses could not crush the clandestine union, but because it often did not operate in the open, the union also could not directly take on the company. The early conflict between the timber companies and the BTW ended in a stalemate.

When workers went on strike, the companies began to use black workers to scab on the union, hoping that fomenting racial resentment, the oldest trick in the Southern anti-unionism playbook, would destroy the movement. But the BTW didn't take the bait. Instead of falling for the trap, the BTW affirmed its commitment to interracial organizing. Big Bill Haywood traveled down to Alexandria, Louisiana, to work with the BTW as it joined the Industrial Workers of the World (IWW). When he addressed the crowd, he grew irate upon finding that the black

BTW workers were meeting separately in accordance with state law, which strictly enforced segregation. To this the labor leader scoffed, "Why not be sensible about this and call the Negroes into this convention? If it's against the law, this is one time when the law should be broken."[119] The black workers were brought into the convention to cheers, and the convention went on to elect its leadership, both black and white. The lumber bosses continued trying to use black strikebreakers to divide the union by race. But the workers of the BTW were schooled in class consciousness. One IWW worker said, "There are white *men,* there are Negro *men,* and there are Mexican *men*, but no 'niggers,' 'greasers' or 'white trash.' All *men* are on the side of the Union."[120]

That was not the only convention the BTW bucked. The BTW extended its membership to local tenant farmers and worked with the Renters' Union of Texas, which, inspired by the work of the BTW, would belatedly begin organizing black and white renters.[121] The BTW also extended membership to the women of the lumber towns. When some questioned this decision, asking whether women should be able to vote on a strike, a BTW man said:

> "A man can go fish and hunt during a strike, but she has to stay at home listening to the babies cry and wondering where the next meal is coming from. Besides, if it weren't for the work of women, many of the men wouldn't hold down jobs. Yes, this is meant to give her a full and equal vote even as to the right to call strikes."[122]

Dues for women were set at $1 a year. Southern men were notoriously difficult to unionize, but the men of the BTW showed a notable tenacity and commitment when on strike.[123] The role of women in the BTW had a large role in that. If a man were to become cowardly or "showed the white feather," the BTW women were said to have threatened their husbands to "Get out of this house and join the union, or I'll leave it, and try to find a man to live with!"[124] When the workers went on strike, women would often join them. If armed thugs or hooligans were sent to attack the striking workers, they first had to look into the eyes of the women of the BTW.

The BTW not only stood to challenge the entrenched power of the bosses; it also represented a new way of living, which conflicted with the racism and patriarchy that had come to dominate the region. To the bosses and those who benefited from the Southern capitalist system, it was a frightening anarchy that needed to be put down with force. To those it held down, however, it was nothing short of liberation.

To stop the spread of the union, men like John Kirby shut down entire sawmilling operations. *The Rebel* responded by petitioning Governor Colquitt to seize the shuttered mills and have the state operate them. Especially egregious to the socialists was the fact that Kirby had stated the reason for shutting down mills was that some of the men in his towns had joined the Socialist Party: "These mill owners assume to dictate to the working class how they shall vote on political questions. This act ... forfeits their right to hold such possession."[125] *The Rebel,* of course, received no reply from the governor. Kirby had been among his earliest supporters, and he intended to dictate how his workers voted and what organizations they could participate in. When

Bill Haywood was set to speak in one of his company towns, Kirby instructed his enforcers to "do everything…to prevent our boys attending… We do not want to put it to them that we are opposed to them doing as they please."[126]

Sometimes, the tactics used to keep men away from BTW speeches were as simple as refusing them access to a church or other suitable venue. One of the benefits of owning a company town is that you can limit who can speak in your town. Kirby even had a barber employed in one of his towns fired for being "pro-union."[127] Other measures were more violent. When an IWW member was set to speak in favor of the Brotherhood of Timber Workers in Jasper, Texas, he was chased off by members of the Ku Klux Klan. A Texas State Senator, E.I. Kellie, wrote to John Kirby about how he kept the radicals out of Jasper: "We told them this was our town." They had no hope of recourse as Kellie and his "boy" "were the law and we would not allow no one [sic] to speak here that preached their doctrine." Adding, "Kellie's 'Old Ku Klux Klan' are [sic] not dead."[128]

Kirby also worked hard to ensure that his black workers stayed in line. He hired one of Texas's great black populist speakers, J.B. Rayner, to address black workers. Rayner was no longer speaking about the "cooperative commonwealth" and the alliance of the working people to take on the money power. Now on the payroll of the "Prince of the Pines," Rayner spoke to black Texans about the "self-help programme" of Booker T. Washington.[129]

Compared to BTW activity in Louisiana, Kirby's firm control over his "feudal towns" allowed him to limit the union's growth in East Texas. But Texas workers did not go quietly, often at high cost to themselves, as well-documented instances of violence and intimidation show. The 1912 Grabow Massacre occurred in Louisiana, where company gunmen opened fire on striking BTW workers, including its leader, Emerson. The company gunmen killed two union workers and an innocent bystander; in self-defense, union men fired back and killed one gunman.[130] A dramatic trial ended in a victory for the BTW, when it was revealed the leader of the gunmen had been encouraging his militia to drink heavily before marching on the striking workers.[131] In Kirbyville, the epicenter of John Kirby's power, forty brave men stood up and walked off the job in solidarity with those massacred by company goons. They were all subsequently fired.[132] This was the future of the Brotherhood of the Timber Workers. Union men were fired and—with the help of a thorough blacklist—shut out of work. Those who stuck around were attacked by company goons.[133] Even, Arthur Lee Emerson, the founder of the BTW, "was severely beaten by Santa Fe guards at Singer in 1913," and "had been driven from the region."

By 1916, the BTW was defeated, but its radical promise lived on. In the 1930s, when the Southern Tenant Farmers' Union continued the tradition of unflinching multiracial unionism, the group cited the bravery and the example of the Brotherhood of Timber Workers, deep in the pineywoods.[134] The Brotherhood of Timber Workers demonstrated the real possibility of a South defined not by race hatred, but by brotherhood, love, and solidarity. A traveler once came across a Brotherhood of Timber Workers meeting. Historian James Green quotes him at length:

I was informed that it was the celebration of Negro emancipation, and that the negroes had given a fine barbecue and that the whites had gone in with them to help out in the financial part and also to celebrate with them as the "Lumber Workers" Union. There were about 2000 or more people upon the ground — about three whites to every two negroes. There was a general mixture of races and sexes, especially when, to the sound of the band, they collected like a swarm of bees — white, black, male and female — around the speaker's stand.[135]

The audience then listened intently to a lecture by a black minister and A.L. Emerson, who connected the fight against slavery to their pitched battle with the timber barons. This was a different path that the South could have taken in the 20th Century. But it was a path that was unacceptable to the rich, like John Kirby, who did everything he could to crush this revolution in the Piney Woods.

Chapter 16

Revolution Crossing The Rio Grande

The ruling class in Texas viewed the Mexican Revolution with horror. Beginning in 1910, sensational stories of peasants not just demanding "tierra y libertad" but seizing it themselves alarmed the landlords and robber barons north of the border. The tenant system in Texas was not so dissimilar from the Mexican hacienda system, and it was not beyond imagination that a similar uprising could happen. For Texas socialists, the Mexican Revolution served as an inspirational and urgent example. If revolution could sweep across Mexico, why not the Lone Star State?

Despite the bolder claims by its leaders to represent all workers, the Texas SP had not yet actively recruited Hispanic Texans into the movement. Much as with black Texans, part of the reason for this was an electoral calculation. In South Texas, Mexican-American votes were effectively controlled by Democratic Party bosses, which provided little incentive for the SP, whose strategy to organize eligible voters led them to forgo organizing amongst disenfranchised groups.[136] However, the most significant reason was the prejudices Anglos held. But just like how the BTW led socialists to reassess their blinkered strategy, the Mexican Revolution demonstrated real-world reasons for recruiting Mexicans into the SP and associated movements.

The Renters' Union benefited immensely from this change in attitude. At the same 1912 convention of the Renters' Union in Waco, where the "radicals" had stripped the "whites only" plank from the group's constitution, the tenant union also praised Emiliano Zapata—a radical leader of the Mexican Revolution and an advocate for radical agrarian reforms—and "identified their cause with the land revolution of the Mexican insurgents."[137] *The Rebel* regularly printed coverage from Zapata, including his 1913 missive addressed to the people of the United States so that they understood the revolution against then Mexican President Francisco Madero.[138] While black membership in the Renters' Union grew slowly, many Mexican Americans joined in this period. The Mexican-American population in Texas was set to double in the 1910s from 125,016 to 251,827.[139] Indeed, these new members were inspired by the radicalism of the Mexican revolution, but they joined the Renters' Union and socialists because of the committed work of figures like F.A. Hernandez.

A tenant farmer born in Nordheim, Texas, to two Tejano parents, F.A. Hernandez understood that the tenant crisis in Texas needed a revolutionary approach.[140] When Hernandez joined up with the Renters' Union, the "new Mexican organizer," as he was called, quickly rose in the ranks as one of its top members.[141] Hernandez had the constitution of the union translated into Spanish so that he could grow the organization with the Mexican renters across Texas.[142] While *The Rebel* proudly reported this, the fact that it took Hernandez's initiative to reach this increasingly militant part of the population in its native tongue shows some of the limitations of the previous commitment of the

Texas SP and Renters' Union to recruiting Mexican Americans to the organization. In any case, Mexican-American membership in the organization grew, and F.A. Hernandez soon joined the Executive Committee of the Renters' Union. By 1915, he became a member of the Texas SP's Literature and Propaganda Committee.[143] As a sign of the changes in the movement, in 1913, at a large gathering for the Renters' Union in Hernandez's hometown of Nordheim, speeches were made in German, English, and Spanish.[144]

In 1912, the Texas SP was the fastest growing socialist party in the country. It added 181 new locals that year; the Renters' Union, which added 4,000 new members in its first year, had played an undeniable role in that.[145] When Hernandez began organizing, the Renters' Union was in the middle of a petition signature drive to be delivered to the Governor of Texas. The petition demanded he call a special session to produce a constitutional amendment in Texas that would "tax all land held for speculation or exploitation . . . to its full rental value" so that "use and occupancy shall become the sole title to land in Texas."[146] If there was any doubt of the inspiration that the Mexican Revolution had on the petition, when it published the petition, *The Rebel* noted the fighting in Mexico and asked, "Have we on this side of the line the intelligence, the character and the spirit to settle this great question of land without bloodshed!"[147] Once again, the Socialists of Texas advocated "ballots not bullets," though the situation in Mexico made the threat clear to the ruling powers in Texas.

The petition was a success, with "fifty thousand signatures from 172 counties."[148] E.R. Meitzen delivered the petition to

Governor Colquitt himself in Austin. The meeting lasted thirty minutes. According to Meitzen, Colquitt dismissed the petition as unrealistic, all while maintaining the ludicrous claim that there were 160 million acres of available land in West Texas, an error *The Rebel* happily noted: "any bright Texas school boy can tell the governor that the total area of Texas … is 170,240,000 acres."[149] His ignorance aside, the governor would never seriously entertain such a radical solution. But as *The Rebel* noted, the petition forced the leader of the Democratic Party:

> "on record as absolutely opposing any radical change from the present system of landlordism that has turned three-quarters of the producing agricultural workers of the state into tenants whose conditions approximates the peonage against which the Mexican people was in rebellion."[150]

As Tom Alter II notes, not only was the move a propaganda victory for Texas socialists, it also raised the land question to prominence in Texas politics. "Before the petition campaign, prohibition was the main issue debated by the candidates for governor. Now…any aspirant for the governor's office who ignored the land issue would do so at their peril."[151] The Renters' Union sought to broaden its appeal at this time, changing its name to the Land League, borrowed from the Irish Land League. The new organization recruited a larger membership base that included "all who pay rent in cities and towns, as well as on farms," wrote an announcement in *The Rebel*. "Landlordism must go."[152]

Much of the revolutionary activity occurred in Northern Mexico but did not stop at the U.S.-Mexico border. Plenty of activity occurred across South Texas and El Paso, and even reached Central Texas. José María Rangel was recruiting Mexicans in Central Texas from Partido Liberal Mexicano (PLM) clubs and among members of the Land League.[153] The group—a throng of armed Mexicans and one white IWW member, Charles Cline—had intended to cross the border into Mexico to fight with Zapata; they wouldn't make it out of Texas. As they made their way to the border, Dimmit County Sheriff Eugene Buck and Deputy Sheriff Candelario Ortiz pursued them.[154] Instead of surrendering themselves to the police, the group captured their pursuers and continued their trek southward. Then, in Carrizo Springs, they were attacked by a group of lawmen from Dimmit County.

The PLM men had no interest in surrender. They took on the lawmen in a gunfight, where two of the PLM men died.[155] The group's leaders, José María Rangel and Charles Cline, were sentenced to life in prison for the murder of Deputy Sheriff Candelario Ortiz, who had been shot while he was held captive.[156] Those arrested were known as Los Mártires de Texas (The Martyrs of Texas), and their case galvanized the IWW and the Socialist movement. The Louisiana socialist Covington Hall's newspaper, *The Voice of The People*, aligned with the IWW, doubted the veracity of the charges against Cline and Rangel: "Their only real 'crime' was in trying to get guns into Mexico... the REAL CRIME of Cline, Rangel and their companion — THEY fought for HUMAN liberty — the others for STANDARD OIL."[157] For its part, *The Rebel*, too, doubted the facts of the case, and questioned whether it was the PLM members who killed Ortiz or the gang that attacked the men as they were on their way to Mexico. Hickey's paper went on to note that the trial, which occurred in San Antonio, was a travesty to the memory of Texas, "in the name of 'the people of Texas' vengeance was demanded against these men who strove in the same cause for which Bowie and Crockett died so splendidly in the fortress Alamo."[158] In 1926, after years of complaint and protest, Texas Governor Miriam Ferguson freed Los Mártires de Texas to Mexico.[159]

Covington Hall and Tom Hickey were ardent defenders and promoters of the Mexican revolution and regularly printed articles from PLM-aligned sources. This camaraderie was reciprocated by the PLM newspaper *Regeneración,* which reported "favorably on the Renters' Union."[160] The Texas SP was firmly committed to protecting the Mexican Revolution from US imperialism. In 1914, the Texas SP platform advocated "a policy of hands off of the internal affairs of Mexico" and "condemned the use of armed forces and other powers" aimed at holding the Mexican "people in bondage."[161] This display of internationalism set the Texas SP apart from its contemporary progressive rivals and served as a counterweight to the pro-war forces brewing in Texas. The violence in Mexico, amplified by sensational coverage of the revolution by an unfriendly Texas press, had convinced many Texans that foreign military intervention was justified. This would play a significant role in ramping up support for the U.S.'s entry in World War I among the general population in Texas.[162]

The Texas SP had distinguished itself against both the Democrats in Texas and the Midwestern and Northern branches of the

Socialist Party as the primary advocate for the landless workers. In Mexico, they witnessed how a revolution could be organized upon those terms. The Mexican Revolution also led to a change in the way many white Texans viewed Mexicans, Mexican Americans, and Tejanos. The demeaning racial stereotypes of the time of the "lazy and servile" Mexican were shown to be laughably wrong. Mexicans were revolutionaries; meanwhile, Texas Anglos were the ones overcome with passivity.

In *The Rebel,* the 1917 Constitution of Mexico was lauded for providing "the entering wedge" in building the "co-operative commonwealth" by attempting to knock "out the two king pins of capitalism, namely RENT and INTEREST."[163] The paper taunted the attitude of racial superiority white Southerners felt toward Mexicans, who had shown themselves more capable of fighting against their oppressors than their neighbors in the United States:

> "Consider the new Mexican constitution ye suckers of the Sunny South who are disposed to sneer at the Mexican, and realize that you have less manhood, backbone and love for your family than the one you called Greaser who fought not to add wealth and power to the Interests that controlled the land resources of his nation, but fought so that he was able to chase them across the Rio Grande, many in their bare feet and in their shirt tails."[164]

The support for Mexico's revolution came at a high cost for Texas socialists, who had already given the state and federal government plenty of excuses to begin their repression against them. The Mexican government had hired the Burns and Sheridan National Detective Agency of New York City to surveil PLM activities in Texas, and they received help from the U.S. Department of Justice, which provided special officers and more coordination with the U.S. marshals in San Antonio.[165] Socialists and IWW members involved with the interracial Brotherhood of Timber Workers were very familiar with the Burns and Sheridan agency, as they had been hired by the timber barons to break the union and acted with impunity.[166] The Texas Rangers were also increasingly involved with subduing the activities of radicals. Following an incident in San Marcos, F.A. Hernandez was arrested on rumors that he and other Mexican Americans were running guns to Mexico. The rumors were false, and Hernandez was released, but Gov Colquitt assigned the Texas Rangers to surveil and suppress those suspected of harboring sympathies to the revolution in Mexico.[167] The American ruling class was heavily invested in Mexico. Texans were no exception; alongside major capitalists like the Rockefellers and J.P. Morgan, familiar antagonists like former Governor Hogg had significant interests in Mexico threatened.[168] Notably, the former Texas Congressman Albert S. Burleson, appointed Postmaster General by Woodrow Wilson, had significant financial interests in Mexico.[169] He deeply opposed the socialists for their support of the Mexican Revolution, their anti-war position, and for embarrassing him by exposing his use of convict labor to forcibly remove tenants from his land.[170] Burleson would play the decisive role in repressing the rights of Texas socialists, ending the Socialist Party of Texas.

The Plan of San Diego gave the Texas Rangers and the federal government the pretense they needed to crack down on the Socialist Party. Named for the town of San Diego, Texas, where the plan was allegedly written, it outlined a scheme to create a "Liberating Army of Races and People" including Mexicans, black people, and the Japanese to take the Southwestern United States from Texas to California.[171] To achieve this, the document called for the execution of all white men over the age of sixteen. This provision led to a race panic amongst white Texans. A raid on a white-owned settlement led to the Texas Rangers engaging in a regime of racial terror across the border, and the deployment of the U.S. Army in the region. Hundreds of Mexicans were killed indiscriminately by the Texas Rangers.

As this hysteria among white Texans increased, the socialist leader E.R. Meitzen, who was running for governor, spoke in Kingsville, Texas, and announced that the people had had plenty to fear. But he wasn't talking about the Plan. Instead, Meitzen pivoted to warn about the owners of the King Ranch, a near-feudal land holding in South Texas larger than the state of Rhode Island. The people needed not worry about Mexican bandits, Meitzen continued, but rather:

> "protection against far more vicious and dangerous bandits—the bandits that hold up a man who is in dire need and rob of his last cent with usurious interest. ... Mexican bandits may be the scum of the earth but they are gentleman and scholars beside the bank bandits that rob only the poor while the border bandits chiefly rob those that have money."[172]

Meitzen was attempting to undercut the growing and frequent appeals to "white solidarity" in Texas, which was a distraction from the real threats to the lives of working-class people, the money power.

There was an effort to "blame the 'Border Troubles' in southwest Texas on the IWW and indirectly the Socialist Party."[173] The Socialist Party, the IWW, and even the PLM had no connection with the Plan of San Diego, but that didn't stop the government from using it as a pretense to try and subdue movements fighting for economic justice in Texas.[174] Soon after, an SP and Land League organizer in San Antonio, giving a public speech to thousands of listeners advocating for "socialism and membership in the land league," was arrested for "inciting a rebellion and insurrection."[175] The brazen attack on freedom of speech and political opponents of the Texas Democratic Party would not stop there. While *The Rebel* did not defend the Plan of San Diego, they continued to defend figures like Pancho Villa and the Mexican Revolution. For example, after Pancho Villa raided Columbus, New Mexico, *The Rebel* promoted a conspiracy that cast doubt on the official reporting that the raid was led by Pancho Villa (it certainly was), claiming that "intervention [in Mexico] is what Wall Street wants."[176]

The conditions in Texas continued to worsen for the Socialists. Despite their successes in recruiting new members, especially among Hispanic Texans, the SP and its associated renters' unions were increasingly targeted. The revolution Hickey had hoped for did not cross the border; there would not be "another Zapata to arise on this side of the Rio Grande."[177] In standing with the Mexican revolutionaries, the Texas socialists had made some friends, but they also had drawn the wrath of the authorities. The Socialists had always maintained they chose "ballots, not bullets" in the class war. It was the U.S. government that would resort to the latter.

Chapter 17

The 1914 Election

In 1914, E.R. Meitzen ran at the top of the ticket for governor. Meitzen had spent his life supporting working-class Texans. His father, E.O. Meitzen, was a veteran of populism, and as the publisher of *The Rebel,* alongside Tom Hickey, Meitzen had come into contact with a long line of radicals. He was a true Marxist. Years later when E.R. Meitzen had passed, his family found a copy of Karl Marx's *Capital* well worn from years of study.[178] However, commitment to political economists, no matter how radical, was not key to socialists' appeal in Texas. That was the land question. Fresh off the successful 1912 election, the socialists believed they would continue to grow in numbers. They had no way of knowing Texas Democrats would nominate a progressive, James "Farmer Jim" Ferguson, to be their gubernatorial candidate.

Farmer Jim was not really a farmer, but a banker. Born on a farm in Bell County, north of Austin, he became a lawyer before marrying the daughter of a well-to-do rancher, Miriam "Ma" Ferguson (who would decades later become the first woman governor of Texas). With her inheritance, James Ferguson eventually owned a bank in Temple, ambling around town with the not-so-folksy help of a chauffeur.[179] James Ferguson understood that politics, tenant farming, and landlordism were major issues in Texas politics, and having "Farmer Jim" in Austin appealed to the toilers of the soil. He also understood how to play political forces against one another. Democratic Party politics at the time was consumed by the question of prohibition. Prohibitionists had endorsed a candidate for the Democratic nomination, and anti-prohibitionist forces in the Democratic Party sought to unite behind one candidate. But because Ferguson refused to identify himself as one or the other—despite having financial ties that made it clear he was no prohibitionist—he was able to side-step the issue, winning the Democratic nomination.[180]

Ferguson was also able to sideline the Socialists. Unlike his predecessor, Colquitt, who waved away the concerns of the Renters' Union, Ferguson included a land plank, including rent reform, in his 1914 campaign, following in the footsteps of former Governor Hogg. His proposal—to limit tenant farmers' rent to "one-third the value of the grain and one-fourth the value of the cotton raise" on rented land—was, to the Texas SP, an attempt to "legalize the exploitative rent," with little other than the equation one uses to calculate rental payments actually changing.[181] But Ferguson understood that by addressing the needs of the farmer, even in such a limited way, he would be able to undermine the Socialists: "take away the abuses of the present rent system and the Socialist would not have a leg to stand on."[182] Ferguson won the election with 175,804 votes, with the Socialists nearly maintaining their 1912 share with 25,083 votes.[183] The Socialists were right about Ferguson's limited interest in the tenant issue; in short order, Ferguson's law was ruled unconstitutional by the Texas Supreme Court and left unaddressed by "Farmer Jim."[184]

While Ferguson had outmaneuvered the Socialists, other factors limited the party's vote total. A new primary law, which required voters to vote for the same party in the general election as they had in the primary, certainly limited the vote for the Texas SP, as some farmers had likely engaged in the Democratic primary to strategically vote for the nominally progressive "Farmer Jim."[185] Meanwhile, landlords and powerful bosses had secured control over elections in their communities. A socialist organizer attested that tenants were intimidated by their landlords "to vote 'right,'" and a federal investigation later found that landlords in Texas cotton country threatened to "raise rents on tenants who voted for increased land taxes" or even evict tenants who "joined the Socialist Party."[186] Investigators also found that lumber barons straddling the border between Louisiana and Texas had ensured that the "secret ballot was a farce." In doing so, socialists and BTW union members were targeted, their resistance quelled. Most brutally, in Groveton, Texas, "one of the best known Socialist speakers in the South," H.L.A. Holman was brutally beaten to death in the street by a company thug while campaigning for the Texas SP.[187] The killer was subsequently bailed out of jail by a group of businessmen.[188] Despite this, working people and tenant farmers continued to organize in and around the Socialist Party.

Chapter 18

War, Betrayal, And The End
Of Texas Socialism

In the 1916 election, the Socialist Party faced similar challenges. At the top of the ticket, Eugene Debs withdrew his name from consideration, creating a void that was later filled by Allan Benson from New York. A more conservative faction of the SP's national body had enjoyed increased power, and sought to limit Debs' influence. The Texas Socialists had hoped to nominate either North Dakotan Arthur LeSeur or Kansas-born Kate Richards O'Hare. But because he was better known among the Northeastern wing of the SP, Benson won the nominating vote.[189] He ran a bore of a campaign. After losing the presidency, he attacked the Socialist Party, claiming it had been overrun with "anarchists" and was "aided and abetted by certain foreigners whose naturalization papers should be canceled."[190]

While frustrated with the presidential campaign, E.R. Meitzen ran again for governor, and Tom Hickey ran for U.S. Senate. Ferguson had not settled the land question and had pivoted toward prohibition, providing what Socialists hoped would be an opening. They campaigned hard on "confiscatory taxes" to promote land reform, and hoped that the land issue they had popularized would provide them with victory. A Houston tax commissioner and Democrat by the name of J.J. Pastoriza, who had "gone as far as the law would allow in taxing real estate at full value," co-wrote a "land amendment" with Hickey promoted by the Socialists.[191] However, the overwhelming focus of the country, the voters, and the socialists was on Europe. The Socialist Party was one of the leading voices opposing U.S. militarism at the advent of World War I. "He kept us out of the war," was a "powerful slogan" according to a prescient article in *The Rebel* predicting a loss to Woodrow Wilson. Comparing Wilson to William Jennings Bryan's run in 1896, *The Rebel* correctly noted Wilson would win "these radical voters" who "are of course not real socialists, but they are that element we always depend upon for converts and gains."[192]

While Socialists campaigned hard, they faced state-led repression and uncertainty among their base on the best course of action to avoid the war. With Wilson's pivot to neutrality undermining the SP platform, and federal reforms aimed at helping farmers, it mattered little how Meitzen campaigned against Ferguson. He tried appealing to the lineage of populism, in a "Red Automobile Tour" with Clarence Nugent, son of renowned populist Thomas Nugent, but it wasn't enough to stave off the national tide. As historian James Green wrote, "Many Socialists cast their votes for Wilson to keep the country out of war rather than voting for Benson to register a protest against capitalism."[193] Thus, socialists weren't able to improve on their previous successes.[194] Democrats, this time at a national level, were able to undermine local and federal SP candidates by offering voters a few choice carrots. Ferguson was reelected governor, Woodrow Wilson was reelected president, and on April 6, 1917, the United States declared war on Germany, officially entering World War I.

Chapter 19

"The Greatest Of All Battles Is On—The Battle For Democracy"

Eugene Debs, speaking to *The Appeal To Reason*, famously said:

> "I have no country to fight for; my country is the earth; and I
> am a citizen of the world… I have not a drop of blood to shed
> for the oppressors of the working class and the robbers of the
> poor, the thieves and looters, the brigands and murderers,
> whose debauched misrule is the crime of the ages, I have a
> heart-full to shed for their victims when it shall be needed in
> the war for their liberation."[195]

Debs perfectly captured the anti-war position of the socialist
movement at the time. Out of a clear-eyed commitment to fighting for the working class, they were unwilling to fight a war
for the benefit of American and European powers. On June 18,
1918, after delivering an anti-war speech in Canton, Ohio, Debs
was arrested and charged with sedition, amid America's first
Red Scare.

* * *

First, they came for *The Rebel*. "Rebel Editor Kidnapped!" read
the top headline of the newspaper's May 26, 1917, edition.[196]

Tom Hickey had been arrested. "Rebels to the front, weaklings to the rear. The greatest of all battles is on—the battle for democracy," *The Rebel* thundered.[197] Before his arrest, Tom Hickey had been surveilled by the Bureau of Investigation, which was looking for ways to suppress anti-war sentiments. After failing to find justification for arresting members of the Meitzen family, they set their sights on Hickey. Opposition to WWI was the focus, but Texas Socialists were being monitored by both federal and Texas authorities.

F.A. Hernandez, who had previously been unjustly arrested in connection with the Mexican Revolution, responded by becoming an informant on anti-war voices, including former comrades in the Texas SP.[198] Hickey was arrested by Texas Rangers and held without a warrant for two days.[199] The government's case against him was entirely fabricated, but a successful conviction was not the point. The arrest was part of a larger operation to spread fear of insurrection and quell any dissent about the draft of WWI.

Hickey was not the only target. The Farmers' and Laborers' Protective Association (FLPA), a new radical farmers' organization aimed at organizing cooperatives and curbing the power of landlords, had been meeting in secret. This was common practice among old American labor organizations to protect members from employer—or, in this case, landlord—retaliation. The FLPA operated out of Eastland, Baylor, Jones, Knox, Hood, Comanche, Erath, and was spreading through West Texas, where tenancy was on the rise. The group also had close ties with similar movements in Oklahoma, such as the radical

Working Class Union, and members would cross the Red River often to collaborate. As frustrated Texas socialists and IWW organizers joined the group, the organization took on a much more radical and militant bent than previous organizations. *The Rebel* claimed the group had "5,000 to 8,000" members and operated in secrecy, including not keeping the names of its members, in order to prevent the landlords, whom the *Rebel* maligned as "interlocked parasites from wielding the boycott and the blacklist... as was the experience of the Renters Union."[200] However, in addition to advocating for tenants' rights, they also opposed conscription, making them a target of the federal government. With little evidence, the feds claimed these farmers were organizing an insurrection against the government. Across Oklahoma and West Texas, FLPA chapters were brutally put down. In Texas, fifty-five people were arrested, almost all of whom were also members of the Socialist Party.[201] The U.S. Attorney General organized the arrests with the help of the U.S. Marshals and Texas Rangers.[202] One member in Mineral Wells, Texas, refused to comply and was killed after lawmen shot him twenty-three times in an armed struggle.[203] In the ensuing trial, due to a lack of evidence, a jury found almost all of the FLPA members innocent, save for three of its leaders.[204] For his part, after his wife paid a $1,000 bond, Tom Hickey was released from Abilene, Texas, having spent two days in custody.

Sensational headlines and stories of sedition and anarchy whipped the public into a frenzy against the socialists. But the government was not done eradicating its political enemies. After being released from confinement, Hickey promised readers of

The Rebel that he would soon expose the assault on democracy and apologized for the limited details in his report, noting:

> "I am writing all this under a sort of censorship that my readers will understand; however, I can definitely promise that the real story will appear in the next Rebel unless I am killed or kidnapped again."[205]

There would be no follow-up, nor would *The Rebel* ever print another issue. The Wilson Administration struck fast and hard. U.S. Postmaster General Albert Burleson, a Texan, landlord, and long-time enemy of the Socialist Party (because it exposed his abuses against tenant farmers on his lands) seized the opportunity to shut *The Rebel* down. Under the auspices of the Espionage Act, enacted in 1917, Burleson made the socialist newspaper the law's first victim. He began this process before the Espionage Act was signed into law.[206] Without the voice and guidance of *The Rebel,* the Socialist Party of Texas collapsed.

Socialism had grown so notably in Texas compared to other states because of the decentralized structure of the state organization. Much of the party organization was local and only connected to the state and national party through publications like *The Rebel. The Rebel* served not just as a newspaper, but as a way for Texas Socialists to communicate with each other across this massive state. Losing this would have been devastating at any time, but it was especially punishing in a moment when prominent socialist leaders had been or were soon to be arrested.

It's worth stating clearly: Texas socialism was not defeated politically. The governments of Texas and the United States effectively made it impossible to be a political radical. After his arrest, Hickey would return to a burned-down barn.[207] Hooligans emboldened by the nationalist fervor had vandalized his property. This was the fate of many of the Socialist Party leaders, who would spend the next few years trying to find some security for themselves, facing head-on the wrath of a rising KKK. Today, most people would be surprised to learn that there *was* a Texas Socialist Party, let alone that it was one of the largest socialist parties in the country. But their quick rise was met with an even quicker collapse. While the leaders would continue trying to revive the spirit of Texas radicalism, the state repression was too much. Tom Hickey would spend the next years trying to relaunch a political newspaper in Texas, but was unsuccessful. There was some hope that the Non-Partisan League could revive the radical spirit in Texas, but it could not overcome the memory of terror and repression.

PART 3

New Deal Blues

Chapter 20

The Pecan Shellers Strike

Emma Tenayuca was better known to her comrades as "La Pasionaria"—the passionate one. Small in stature, with piercing eyes and a fiery commitment to justice, she would lead one of the largest strikes in Texas history.

Tenayuca was born in San Antonio in 1916, in the midst of the first Red Scare, which saw the Texas Socialist Party all but collapse. Her family had deep roots in the region; they had arrived in 1723, just five years after a Spanish expedition officially founded what was then a colonial outpost along the banks of the San Antonio River. If any city can lay claim to representing Texas history, it's San Antonio, home of the Alamo. Developing into a major hub during Spanish and Mexican rule, all kinds of people crossed paths there. When the Anglo newcomers took over, the city became known for its brutal mistreatment of Tejanos. Consider, for example, another San Antonian, Juan Seguín. Born in San Antonio in 1806, Seguín spent his life in service to his home of Texas: He was a hero of the Texas Revolution, a courier from the battle of the Alamo who also fought at the Battle of San Jacinto, where General Sam Houston decisively defeated Mexico's forces led by Santa Anna. From 1837 to 1849, he even served as a senator in the Republic of

Texas. However, after the revolution, Seguín's status as a war hero couldn't save him from the frenzied Anglo mobs, who questioned the loyalty of a man who had organized the burial for his fallen comrades at the Alamo. Eventually, they made it so dangerous for Seguín and his family that he fled his home for Mexico.[1] Seguín would eventually return to Texas, to be buried in his home state, but his story is one of the many crimes perpetrated against Tejanos and Mexican Americans in Texas.

For decades, South Texas held a reputation for white mob violence, while Democrats' political bosses outright controlled the vote through corruption and bribery. The Populists failed to substantially organize there, and the Socialists, while inspired by the Mexican Revolution, only began building relationships with Mexican-American workers shortly before their political demise. Despite these failures, Emma Tenayuca would channel the lessons and tradition of this movement, leading one of the most important strikes in Texas history—the Pecan Shellers Strike of 1938.

Nearly one hundred years after Juan Seguín was chased from his home, Tenayuca stood with thousands of workers, some born in the United States and some migrants. Eventually, facing mob violence, she would be forced to flee to California. Still, like Juan Seguín, Emma would eventually return home to Texas, where she remains a symbol of working-class power and resistance. In a speech decades later, Tenayuca would say of her work as an organizer, "I never felt like a foreigner, certainly with an Indian name like Tenayuca, I am indigenous and so are a lot of people to this region."[2]

* * *

Texas was blessed with a bounty of pecan trees, and pecans became a big business. Between 1927 and 1936, Texas produced "an average of 22,543,000 pounds of seedling pecans per year," totaling nearly half of all seedling pecans in the country.[3] The work of shelling those pecans was done in San Antonio. To gain an advantage over its competition, the Southern Pecan Shelling Company revamped its production process, not by mechanizing production but by removing machinery. Because of the ongoing depression, the company knew it could pay Mexican-American laborers in the area pauper wages, which would be much cheaper than buying and maintaining machinery.[4]

At the time, Mexican-American workers faced not only abuse from bosses, but also police harassment and weaponized deportations. Even American citizens were not safe from the threat of indiscriminate deportations, with border patrol threatening and even beating several Mexican-American workers in retaliation for their organizing.[5] The Southern Pecan Shelling Company's business model, then, was based on the super-exploitation of San Antonian labor, paying pecan shellers five to seven cents per pound, and pecan crackers around fifty cents per one hundred pounds. For workers, who technically worked as contract laborers—some shelling at home but most in large subcontractor facilities[6]—this averaged out to about four or five cents per hour.[7]

The company profited heavily from the arrangement, becoming one of the more successful pecan manufacturers in the country. The many subcontract facilities claimed they were independent, but in reality they were "financed and controlled" by larger companies.[8] Pecan shellers worked long days—often 75-hour weeks—in crowded rooms with little to no ventilation. The dust from thousands of pecans would fill the air, and workers suffered high rates of tuberculosis.[9] Their living conditions were often just as dire: Only twenty-five percent had electricity, and only nine percent had running water.[10] FDR's National Recovery Administration investigated the situation and determined that current wages were "an insult to any human being." The agency proposed new wage standards for the industry of 15 cents an hour. For comparison, the Monthly Labor Review found in 1936 that the average hourly entry-level wage for male "common laborers" in Texas was around 40 cents for whites, 33 cents for black workers, and 30 cents for male Mexican laborers. The national average across race and region for this work was 43 cents an hour.[11] In any case, the new NRA standard was effectively impossible to enforce because of workers' contract classification. In fact, the NRA didn't attempt to enforce these rules at all.[12] Likely emboldened after the FDR administration failed to act, the Southern Pecan Shelling Company announced[13] it would slash all workers' wages even further.[14] In response, around twelve thousand pecan shellers went on strike. They were led by the young Emma Tenayuca.

Though Tenayuca was just 21 when the strike occurred, she had already earned the trust of her community. Her nickname, "La Pasionaria," was a fitting one for a woman first arrested when she was still a teenager. In 1933, when around four hundred workers, mostly young Mexican women, at the Fink Cigar factory went on strike, the police had no issue with making a violent spectacle. As Emma Tenayuca herself recalled in a 1983 interview with the *Texas Observer*, the local sheriff, Albert West, "had a picture taken of himself with a brand new pair of boots. He said that was what was going to greet the [Fink factory] strikers."[15] Young Emma Tenayuca, who was not employed at the factory, went to the picket line anyway to show solidarity, and she and others were arrested. After graduating from high school, she got a job as an elevator operator at the Gunter Hotel and got busy organizing.[16]

The legacy of the Mexican Revolution, Texas socialists, and the IWW was still well known on the streets of San Antonio. Young Emma received her education in radical ideas at Milam Park— then known as Plaza del Zacate—where speakers stood on soapboxes to deliver speeches about a coming socialism and workers' revolution.[17] Tenayuca looked first toward the Socialist Party— which still existed nationally but had all but disintegrated in Texas—whose speakers had inspired her as a young girl, but the movement in Texas had turned from a radical class-rooted organization into a talk shop after attending a few Socialist Party meetings, where the members argued amongst each other about Russia, Trotsky, and other topics seemingly a world away from the needs of working people in San Antonio. "I didn't get anything from that," Tenayuca told the *Texas Observer* years later.[18] Soon, she joined the Communist Party, one of the few organizations that sought to organize with Mexican-American workers (though in much more limited way, compared to their work organizing black workers across the South).[19] She even co-wrote theory in *The Communist*, the party's journal, with her husband, Homer Brooks. She read widely, including Marx's *Value, Price, and Profit* and *Wage Labour and Capital*, but felt no need to lie, unlike many others, about tackling Marx's tome *Das Kapital*.[20] Through the CP-USA, she organized with the Workers Alliance of America, an offshoot of the Socialist Party and Communist Party attempts at organizing jobless workers.[21] In that role, she advocated for Mexican Americans to be included in the relief programs from the federal government, demanding fairer distribution from the Works Progress Administration, and advocated for relief programs for children.[22]

Tenayuca had the commitment of a radical, without the dogmatism. Describing her politics, she recounted a moving scene she witnessed in which a worker from the city, with no prior experience in agriculture, was picking tomatoes too slowly to meet the boss's daily quota. So, one by one, other workers added a tomato to his basket. By the end of the day, he not only met the quota but also received permission to take some of the excess home for himself. This scene reminded her "it was possible to be human." "The idea of sharing, of helping — this was brought into the Communist movement. You could see it in the labor struggle."[23]

* * *

When the pecan shellers went on strike, they asked Emma Tenayuca to help. Her role with the Workers' Alliance had proven to her community that she could be trusted; when it was time to strike, she was unanimously selected to lead, the crowd chanting her name: "Emma, Emma, Emma!"[24]

On February 1, 1938, thousands of workers went on strike, walking off their jobs, and formed picket lines across 170 pecan shelling factories.[25] Soon the strike would grow to include 10,000 of workers. The strike would continue for three months, interfering with the peak season for pecan shelling. They were met with severe police resistance. The political establishment in San Antonio wanted the strike over and the police were happy to oblige. To justify their mass arrests, San Antonio police cited a rule that prevented the carrying of advertising signs without the permission of the City Marshal.[26] There were also official complaints that the picketers were blocking sidewalk traffic, which was meant to justify the unjustifiable: Striking workers were beaten by police and firefighters armed with clubs for standing on the sidewalk. This seemingly minimal infraction came with a large fine for pecan shellers—$15—most of whom made less than $3 a week.[27] Those who could not pay the fine were held in inhumane conditions. With little regard for human rights or dignity, the police stuffed eighteen people, side by side, into a jail cell designed for only four people. At another facility, two hundred and forty strikers were stuffed into a cell with a sixty-person capacity. When they cried in anguish, the police chief, Owen Kilday, sprayed "a fire hose into the cell."[28]

A district judge was confronted with a suit from the strikers, who rightfully argued the police were infringing upon their rights. Judge S.G. Tayloe ruled that the strikers had a right to picket but did not have a right to disobey the laws being arbitrarily enforced by the police.[29] In addition to the police threats, the ruling elites used threats of deportation to try to quell striking workers. Emma Tenayuca noted how this was used during the 1933 cigar strike; a local politician had even claimed that "all he had to do was notify the immigration authorities and they would go to the picket line."[30] But the strikers persevered, and while the police crackdowns grew more violent, the workers had support from the community.[31] Emma never wavered, with a keen focus on organizational details. While Emma Tenayuca was regularly present—and arrested—on the picket lines, she spent nights coordinating with other strike leaders about where to send people, encouraging and inspiring community members to show up in spite of the crackdowns, and ensuring that they were prepared for what would come. She was always sure to keep the workers at the center of the movement; after all, they were the ones with her also on the front lines. Years later, she modestly said of her pivotal role, "The only thing I did was organize these committees and send them down. The first thing was to prepare for a meeting and to keep the workers out [on strike]."[32] Tenayuca is known as a hero, but she was not one to chase the spotlight.

The government saw this young 21-year-old as a significant threat. San Antonio Mayor C.K. Quin was particularly worried about Tenayuca's influence, as was police chief Owen Kilday, who told Edwin A. Elliott, regional director of the then-new National Labor Relations Board, "If the strike is won under present leadership, 25,000 workers on the West Side [of San Antonio] would fall into the Communist Party."[33] Not wanting her leadership of the strike to divert attention from the workers' demands, Tenayuca resigned as the leader.[34] She was more interested in the strike's success than in her position. Years later, she said of the leadership change, "We had not developed the leadership to take care of the negotiations ... I knew that I was a good organizer ... this was something else."[35] She may have stepped down as the leader, but she spent her time meeting with picket captains and drafting memorandums, the thankless work at the heart of organizing. Most days, she could still be found on the picket lines, inspiring those around her. As the labor leader Latane Lambert said of Tenayuca, "It was right she would be called La Pasionara because in her shrill little voice she would make your spine tingle."[36]

The Committee for Industrial Organization (CIO), under the leadership of Donald Henderson, took over the strike from Tenayuca, with her support.[37] While San Antonio politicians and the police may have had their blanket suspicions of any union leader, it was not then known if he was a member of the Communist Party. But Henderson had, years before, tried to pressure H.L. Mitchell, founder of the Southern Tenant Farmers' Union, to join the party in secret.[38] Despite the efforts of Police Chief Kilday, Henderson was able to get many pecan shellers to affiliate with the CIO. He refused to negotiate with city officials, instead demanding to speak directly with the company and representatives from the Department of Labor.[39] The police chief continued to egregiously overstep his authority. The CIO had sent another organizer to San Antonio, J. Austin Beasley, whom Kilday immediately arrested, claiming he was wanted in El Paso.[40] The justification was completely fabricated, but it was fitting for a police chief who said, when challenged by a union leader for his unconstitutional and anti-labor tactics, "It is my duty to interfere with revolution and communism is revolution."[41]

The gangster-like activity of the police chief garnered national and international attention, leading the Governor of Texas, James Allred (who also happens to be a distant relative of 2024

Senate candidate Colin Allred), to get involved.[42] The governor got the union and the company to agree to arbitration, and the Texas Industrial Commission investigated the activities of the police chief, finding that he acted unlawfully.[43]

Kilday and the police had not only bent the law to arrest strikers for picketing; they'd also shut down soup kitchens, hoping that hunger would force strikers back to work, and used the threat of deportations to force Mexican workers to return to work.[44] But the workers of San Antonio held out, and the union negotiated a temporary compromise on wages of seven and eight cents, with the promise that negotiations would continue.[45] When Congress passed the Fair Labor Standards Act of 1938, implementing a minimum wage of twenty-five cents an hour, the pecan industry tried to organize a carve-out, claiming that their work was "agricultural" and should be exempted.[46] The CIO supported the company, fearing that the change would otherwise result in job losses. In any case, the company brought back the machines to automate the work, and pecan shelling ceased to be a major employer in the city.

* * *

While Emma Tenayuca is well-respected by many, she is not as widely known as she should be. For example, in a 2019 video for the Texas State Historical Society, Dr. Emilio Zamora noted his surprise that she did not have an entry in the TSHA Handbook of Texas until 2016.[47] In recent years, following the progressive insurgency, and as interest in U.S. labor history, particularly the role of women, has grown, there has been renewed interest in Tenayuca. This is a good thing. Her impact on Texas and labor history is undeniable. Not only were the strikes notable for their size, but many of the strikers were also women and immigrant workers who showed the world their power. Their fight was about wages, but it was also a demand for dignity against the whims of the company, the government, and the police.

From her education at Plaza del Zacate, Tenayuca was deeply connected to Texas's radical history and the Mexican revolutionary tradition that had such a deep impact on the Lone Star State. Among the speakers were anarcho-syndicalists, who remembered the time of the Renters' Union and the Land League: Old IWW veterans who had likely read the fiery essays of Tom Hickey in *The Rebel* and condemned the murderers of their Brotherhood of Timber Workers comrades in the Grabow Massacre. In this way, her legacy connects back to the People's Party, which was born from William Lamb's commitment to connect labor with political action. In 1886, William Lamb had argued that tenant farmers and the Knights of Labor would need to join together to take on the ruling class economically and electorally, because the political system and the economic system were rigged against them. Nearly a hundred years later, with the hindsight and knowledge of what became of the People's Party, the Socialist Party, and the labor movement, Tenayuca said:

> "[T]he American system has fought tenaciously and viciously against the organization of labor. On the other hand, ... if labor had accepted the Socialist Party, I think you would have still had a large Socialist Party here. The idea of socialism, the idea of a cooperative society still exists. Who's going to begin it here?"[48]

This question lingers today. Following the strikes, Emma Tenayuca continued her involvement with the Communist Party, eventually becoming Chairwoman of its Texas chapter. In August 1939, she held a rally for the party with the permission of then-Mayor Maury Maverick. Five thousand Texans, whipped up into a frenzy against communism, violently broke into the building, at which point Emma and others had to escape through tunnels underneath.[49] Protesters even burned an effigy of the mayor outside City Hall. The threats on her life became too great, and she fled to Houston before eventually moving to California.[50] Soon, she became disillusioned with the Communist Party, claiming she could never understand the German-Soviet Nonaggression Pact.

Still, she maintained her commitment to socialism and the working class. Years after the Pecan Shellers Strike, she was still thinking like a radical. She rejected theories that some sustained crisis would result in a naturally occurring workers' revolution—ideas which were especially popular among intellectuals in the lead-up to the Second World War. Instead, she argued that socialism was something to be built through education, by and through people engaging with one another collectively:

> "I have never looked upon socialism or upon social democracy as coming about suddenly as the result of a crisis. I look upon it as an educational endeavor, where people learn to work together, where they learn to think together."[51]

Accelerationists, as they are known today, believe that once conditions have deteriorated enough, the common people will simply "wake up" and join revolutionary movements for change. History has shown this to be a fantasy. It is an inherently pessimistic view of people, their capacity for understanding, and their willingness to take action—the polar opposite of socialism. Fundamentally, socialism is an optimistic philosophy. It has plenty of criticism for the world as it currently exists, but this criticism comes from an optimistic belief that a better world is possible. It is this optimism that allows everyday people to stand up and bravely meet their moment in history. It is this optimism that inspired a young 21-year-old woman to face down the police, the bosses, and the government without blinking—and for thousands of working people to follow suit.

A Texas radical, a socialist, believes in the capacity of everyday people and understands their role not as merely "waking up" the sleeping masses, but as providing them with tools, organization, and the support necessary to take on the monumental challenge of making a better world. Emma Tenayuca was many things, but she was undoubtedly a Texas radical—maybe even one of the last, at least, of a certain kind. In this radical period from Reconstruction to the New Deal, generation after generation of Texans rose to fight for a better future, for a "cooperative commonwealth." More importantly, they built organizations of working people—like the Farmers' Alliance, The People's Party, the Socialist Party, and the Brotherhood of Timber Workers— which all, in their own way, concluded that to achieve their goals, they would need to build independent movements of the working class. Most crucially, they understood that to achieve their goals, and engage in politics, they would need to take on the power of the capitalist class.

Each of these movements was brutally put down, but in their collapse, another emerged armed with the lessons from the past and schooled in the distinct tradition of Texas radicalism. This Texas radicalism was the common-sense answer to a world turned upside-down. When Texas populist S.O. Daws asked why "those who work most get least, and those who work least get most," he was, perhaps unwittingly, laying the groundwork for future Texas socialists. Each encampment—bringing together thousands of Texas farmers for political discussions and merriment—was, in a way, planting the seed for the *next* encampment, building a tradition. This radicalism continued through the Brotherhood of Timber Workers, and through Emma Tenayuca's organizing, as she tried to revive those same ideals she had discovered while listening to the old Socialist Party veterans speak of the "cooperative commonwealth." She fought to remake those movements, and expand those promises to Tejano and Mexican-American workers, and to immigrants too often forgotten. But the first and second Red Scare—the first, around World War I, which destroyed the Socialist Party; and the second, in and after World War II—chased radicals like Tenayuca out of the state, and left an indelible mark on what came next. How much of the tradition could survive?

Of course, there would be socialists, radicals, and labor leaders. And many Texans to come would know and keep the knowledge of these earlier movements alive. There would be many important and successful social movements, such as the Civil Rights movement, the anti-war movement, and the fight for immigrant justice, which achieved much in the way of dignity and justice for Texans. But capitalism no longer would be the direct target of these movements in the same way. It was an understandable development; our history shows those in power have no tolerance for this kind of movement. But the thread connecting the populists' and the socialists' traditions—kept alight through the radical traditions of the Mexican Revolution, the veterans of socialism, and the IWW—was violently severed.

It can be rebuilt. Organizations like the Democratic Socialists of America are once again asking questions like S.O. Daws', and they've won offices in cities like Austin and San Antonio. It is an open question if DSA will be able to reconnect with the working-class as a whole in Texas; recent years have only seen a further rightward electoral shift in the state. But the idea of the "cooperative commonwealth" still exists. As Tenayuca asked, we must ask anew: "Who's going to begin it here?"

Conclusion

For most of its history, the Democratic Party dominated all procedures in the Texas State Capitol. Even the political movements that started outside the party structure were absorbed into it. Progressives, conservatives, reformers, and redeemers all would battle for control from within the party apparatus. Yet, today, a Democrat has not won statewide office in more than 30 years. This is the longest electoral drought for a state Democratic Party in all fifty states. How did Republicans so thoroughly reshape Texas politics?

The story often goes that the GOP unseated Democrats because Lyndon B. Johnson signed the Civil Rights Act. This idea is often buttressed by an LBJ quip, as recalled by his assistant: "Well, I think we may have lost the south for your lifetime—and mine."[1] But this presumes that the parties simply "flipped," and while the Civil Rights Act forever reshaped American politics, especially at the national level, this doesn't fully explain how the uniparty failed to adapt to the moment as it had previously.

Nearly three decades passed between the Civil Rights Act's passage and the GOP's complete Texas takeover. It remained something of a swing state in presidential elections, hopping from Richard Nixon in 1972 to Jimmy Carter in '76 before attaching itself to Ronald Reagan in the '80s. Bush Sr., a Texan, had worse voter margins in his home state than in states like Virginia,

Georgia, or Mississippi, although he still won by some 13 points. (Texans had rejected Bush Sr. in three previous statewide races, for senator in 1964 and 1970, and the 1980 Republican presidential primary.) It was only after the 1992 election that Texas revealed itself to be a solid Republican state. Why?

Texas, at the local level, had staggered into a period of true party competition. There had always been political factions in Texas politics, even during periods of uniparty rule—recall the Populist leaders who joined with Democrats to pass watered-down versions of their reforms. This had been beneficial for the Democrats' liberal bloc, harmful to its conservative flank. The conflict between the Texas Democrats' two major factions had festered since the 19th century, with both sides trading blows over the years. But in the post-war period, it exploded into the open; suddenly, Democratic apparatchiks were roping in the Republican Party.

Doing so wasn't totally new: conservative Democrats had previously sought endorsements from national Republicans (Allan Shivers, a Democratic governor from 1949 to 1957, was once even cross-nominated as a Democrat and a Republican, topping the ticket for both parties) while liberal Democrats made strategic choices to oppose their party's conservative bloc. In the 1961 special election to fill LBJ's Senate seat after he became vice president, Democrat William A. Blakley ran against Republican John Tower. The conservative Democrat was seen as so unacceptable to liberal Texans that many considered doing the unthinkable: voting Republican. The *Texas Observer*, the voice of Texas liberalism, even endorsed Tower over Blakley.

In its endorsement, the *Texas Observer* argued, "liberals want to free their party from the dead weight of the Dixiecrats," and "Republicans want to re-orient Texas conservatism into a source of greater national GOP strength."[2] If there were a viable conservative party in Texas, the conservatives in the Democratic Party could be forced out, and real political competition would come to Texas. Tower's victory would mean the "Texas GOP would have a tremendous prestige factor to aid their rising organization," and if Blakley were to win, it would waste "a golden opportunity for reform of the archaic party institutions with which the political climate of Texas has been too long shrouded."[3] Texas liberals got their wish; John Tower won his election by a narrow margin of about 10,000 votes out of nearly a million cast. Though Democrats would continue to dominate the state for years after the 1961 special election—albeit with its conservative and liberal wings still fighting bitterly—the Republican Party was becoming a viable alternative.

Politics was not the only thing changing in Texas. The oil industry was in decline. Just as the cotton industry's decline led to significant changes in the populist era, the oil slump reorganized much of the Texas economy. From 1981 to 1991, the petroleum industry was cut in half; meanwhile, employment in the Texas oil industry declined by one-third. White and blue-collar workers were all swept up in the firings and downsizing of the industry.[4] At the same time, Texas agriculture was again in crisis (along with farmers in the rest of the country), where the cost of production suddenly outstripped the prices of the farmers' products. (The farmers found a voice in the progressive agriculture commissioner Jim Hightower, who served for eight years.)

Meanwhile, Texas experienced significant population growth, with people from out of state relocating to Texas to work in its growing white-collar sectors. Many of these people were relocated by their companies and settled in the Texas suburbs, which would become a bulwark of Republican power. These new voters, unlike native-born Texans, didn't hesitate to identify with the Republicans they had back home. In 1985, forty-one percent of these new arrivals in Texas identified as Republicans, compared to just twenty-eight percent of native-born Texans.[5] Compared to other Southern states, the migration of Republican voters from other states played a significant role in "the growth of Republican identification" in Texas. So did defections. In 1990, with Karl Rove advising his campaign, a State Representative by the name of Rick Perry switched parties and ran as a Republican against Jim Hightower for the position of Texas Agriculture Commissioner.[6] By casting his opponent as a "far-out left-winger,"[7] Perry defeated Hightower, launching his career as a statewide politician and becoming a household name. (He would later serve as the Governor of Texas for fourteen years.)

Elsewhere in the Capitol, 1990 was a good year for Texas liberals. Ann Richards became the second woman to be elected governor, sparking hope—despite Hightower's defeat—that there might be a place for liberal politics in the state. She was a widely popular governor, but Karl Rove saw that Texas was trending more Republican and took advantage. In 1994—a national red wave year—George W. Bush made Richards a one-term governor, and while other Democrats won their statewide races that year, Republicans would sweep practically every election from then on out.

When looking at Ann Richards' failed reelection, people often cite a few things: First among them is Bush's name-brand recognition, but Richards had also vetoed a concealed carry bill. Following 1991 a mass shooting at a Luby's Cafeteria in Killeen, which was at the time one of the worst shootings in U.S. history, the Texas Legislature had passed a bill allowing those 21 and older without a criminal background to conceal carry. Ann Richards vetoed it, saying, "The only outcome of the passage of this bill will be more people killed by gunfire." Following the Siege of Waco, in which the U.S. Government left 126 dead, including 42 children, Richards also reportedly said she would "seriously consider" an assault weapons ban in Texas.[8] Broadly speaking, this is why she was often labeled too "socially liberal" to win again.

She also came up against the growing influx of new Republican voters. Her campaign press secretary, Chuck McDonald, later reflected on the campaign, saying a significant factor was the white-collar jobs she had brought to Texas. "Southwestern Bell in San Antonio, big telecom companies in North Texas, all the growth in Round Rock. The growth in suburban areas...was phenomenal. Those people voted Republican."[9]

In the next decades, demographics became the obsession for Democrats from top to bottom. Since Bill Clinton and the implementation of the North American Free Trade Agreement, or NAFTA, the Democratic Party has essentially embraced the dealignment of working-class voters from the party. NAFTA—which Richards strongly supported—played an outsized role in Democrats losing working-class and rural voters across the United States, and it had a big effect on Texas. Between 1994 and 2010, Texas lost half of its manufacturing jobs in the private sector, from 16.2 percent to 8.4 percent.[10] Much of this was in South Texas, the part of the state Democrats are losing to the Right. Instead of providing an alternative to the Republican Party, Democrats tried to pivot from the politics of Ann Richards and Jim Hightower to figures like Henry Cuellar, an anti-abortion Democrat from South Texas favored by party leaders like Nancy Pelosi. While Democrats maintained small fiefdoms in urban parts of the state, GOP rule at the state level has for decades maneuvered to limit their power.[11]

Still, there was hope that demographic shifts, like those that brought Republicans into power, would change Democrats' fortune—the aforementioned "demographics as destiny" argument. In 2024, the idea that non-white voters were just Democrats in waiting exploded in Democrats' faces—both statewide and nationally. No amount of blogs or op-eds on the potential for a demographically-induced upset in 2024 could make up for the utter lack of spending from the national party in communities such as South Texas.[12] Instead, the DNC funneled millions into swing states like Georgia, Pennsylvania, and North Carolina (they were routed in all three), and only deigned to visit Texas days before the election, for an ill-advised rally in Houston featuring Beyoncé.[13]

When it comes to making Texas "competitive," the national Democratic Party has one story for the media and another behind closed doors. What does exist in Texas on the Democratic Party side is a host of competing PACs that increasingly feud with local Texas Democratic Party chapters.[14] While these PACs operate with varying levels of success and can, in theory, be more effective, they exist at the whims of their donors; leaders rise and fall according to which way the wind blows. When the Republicans looked to reshape Texas, they invested seriously in developing cadres and in youth organizations.[15] The Texas Democratic Party is retracting, not growing. In 2022, the party had a vacancy at the county chair level in 30 percent of Texas rural counties and 10 percent in suburban and urban counties.[16] For comparison, Republicans had zero vacancies. There's ample evidence that another path is possible. While Bernie Sanders lost Texas in the 2020 Democratic Primary, he did best among Hispanic voters, many of whom went for Trump in 2024.[17] There's a path out of GOP control of Texas, but it will require a commitment to economic populism and bottom-up organizing that reaches folks outside of corporate PACs' voter spreadsheets. For now, though, Democrats seem much more interested in raising money for money's sake.

* * *

> "The present system of production and exchange puts the greed of one set of men against the humanity of another set of men; it puts dividends above human lives and magnifies the dollar as of more consequence than the honor of men, the virtue of women, or the innocence of children."[18]

These words were from G.G. Hamilton, the fiery preacher who set out to debate socialism and found himself converted to its cause. He was one of many who sought solidarity and collective action to fight for a better Texas. These were people in desperate circumstances. In a letter to Tom Hickey, one mother wrote, "This is a beautiful country, full of poverty and starvation."[19]

One thing you may have noticed is that every group in this book lost. The Populists came close to power but collapsed in a matter of years. The Socialists fought hard but were unable to withstand state repression in response to the Mexican Revolution and World War I. The Brotherhood of Timber Workers was crushed. The Pecan Shellers Strikers were sold out; the cowboy strikers were run out of town; the fence cutters were jailed or worse. All were defeated. Is that the tradition of Texas radicalism?

It's difficult to take the long view when so much is at stake. But without a doubt, each of these movements left its mark on Texas and American history. The fight for the open range and the idea of the commons became the struggle for a cooperative commonwealth. The populists and socialists helped create the basis of the labor movement, the New Deal, and over a century later, the Bernie campaign. These movements were more than lobbying efforts; they flowed into each other, inspiring future movements and building on the mistakes of the past.

What is notable about the history of Texas radicalism is not that it existed, but that it ceased to exist. Throughout this period in Texas history, each generation took up the question of inequality, capitalism, and democracy. Even in defeat, these working-class movements would reorganize themselves and launch another fight for the cooperative commonwealth. But after the defeat of the Socialist Party, this tradition was never able to revive itself. Its tradition lived on in individuals, but the mass movement that once brought thousands to the summer encampments would not return. Since then, there have been important struggles in Texas: the labor movement, the Civil Rights movement, the fight for gay rights, and today, the struggle to end the genocide of Palestinians. When the Civil Rights Movement started to advocate for economic justice, the state brutally crushed it, and during the second Red Scare, radicals were purged from labor unions. The problems that these radicals faced continue today. Universities in Texas have been at the forefront of a chilling crackdown on free speech, from students protesting the genocide in Gaza being beaten by police to the state-mandated review of syllabi at public universities. Dr. Thomas Alter II, whose work on the Texas Populists and socialists is frequently cited in this book, was fired from his position at Texas State University for speaking at a socialist conference in his own free time.

Texas is a state of extreme wealth inequality. While the state amends its constitution to ban wealth taxes, it faces some of the highest food insecurity[20] and poverty rates[21] in the country. While the state strips workers of basic protections like water breaks, sixty-six billionaires earn more in a year than more than three-fourths of state residents.[22] In the tradition of lumber baron John Kirby, Elon Musk, today's richest man in the world, has set up his own company town, Starbase, in South Texas; he has the governor of Texas on speed dial.[23] While Democrats continue to fumble in the dark, the question for today's radicals is not whether to continue fighting, but how. Decades ago, as Ronald Reagan destabilized millions of people's lives, Emma Tenayuca said, "The idea of socialism, the idea of a cooperative society still exists. Who's going to begin it here?"[24]

* * *

Following Bernie's defeat in 2016, the Democratic Socialists of America, or DSA, grew from a small and isolated organization into a major political force, working in coalition with progressive groups and labor unions. In Texas, there are active chapters from the Rio Grande Valley to Lubbock, with endorsed city council members in Austin and Corpus Christi, and three card-carrying DSA city council members in San Antonio. DSA plays a major role in local politics in Texas's largest cities, Greg Casar's meteoric rise from DSA member and Policy Director of the Workers' Defense Project—a group organizing for immigrant and worker justice, combating wage theft and other abuses faced by vulnerable workers—to the Austin City Council, to now serving as the Chair of the Progressive Caucus in Congress is a testament to the growing electoral strength of the movement. However, the fact that he came out of DSA but is no longer endorsed by the organization—over disagreements surrounding his past statements on Palestine—is a testament to another challenge. How can the organization maintain its victories while staying true to its membership and core principles?

Texas ranks near the bottom of the country in union density, with around 4.5 percent registered union membership (the national average is 10 percent). But there are very encouraging signs of growth. Between 2022 and 2024, Texas added 68,000 new union members, driven in large part by the historic organizing drives at Starbucks, along with growth in Texas's technology sector.[25] And the unions folks are joining are much more committed to bold radical change. In 2021, the Texas AFL-CIO, with sizeable membership in the oil and gas industry, endorsed a major climate plan, including a just transition.[26] And in January of 2024, the Texas AFL-CIO became the first state labor organization to endorse a ceasefire in Gaza.[27] In Texas's major cities, largely run by the Democratic Party, unions play an outsized role in local politics, with politicians competing amongst each other for their coveted endorsements.

These are encouraging signs. But Texas today is still far from the kind of organization of working people found at the height of Texas radicalism. As it currently exists, the Texas left, much like the broader U.S. left, is much more "class-focused" than it is "class-rooted," as the political theorists Sam Gindin and the late Leo Panitch have argued, borrowing from trade unionist Andrew Murray. The difference is key. Left populists like Bernie Sanders and Jeremy Corbyn opened the political conversation up to broader discussions of class, but *discussions* of class are different from *class movements*. Class-focused politics don't emerge from the organic institutions of the class itself, nor does it advance the socialist perspective of the class for itself.[28] Currently, the U.S. Left is a loose association between progressives, democratic socialists, and NGOs. It can win essential reforms, but it will not be able to mobilize the working class as a whole to become its own political agent. The challenge we face today is how to translate the broad discontent people feel into class-rooted working-class organizations that are capable of taking on the ruling class. Democratic socialism is about democracy, both political and economic, and socialists should be concerned with putting power into the hands of everyday people. It can be built, but it doesn't currently exist.

As Sam Gindin once wrote, capitalism has created a working class that is, "fragmented, particularist, employer-dependent, pressured by its circumstances to be oriented to the short term, and too overwhelmed to seriously contemplate another world."[29] This, of course, benefits capitalists the most. In Texas, part of the work required to build working-class institutions will be reconnecting with our radical roots. The Farmers' Alliance and later the People's Party were "class-rooted" forms of politics, where working people came together not only to act but to learn and decide together what needed to change. When the Democratic establishment was unwilling to implement the common-sense, class-rooted demands of the farmers, these poor and forgotten farmers were able to build a movement that forever changed this state's politics. And the class-rooted nature of these organizations gave them the strength to withstand many of the assaults and setbacks that those looking to challenge the power of the rich will face. Even in defeat, these movements laid the groundwork for American liberalism and saw many of their demands achieved in the decades that followed.[30]

I often return to how Eugene Debs euphorically described the socialist encampments across Texas and Oklahoma. "These rugged tillers of the soil who have endured all things and are yet patient and strong, and with the light Socialism shining in their honest faces they are transfigured and to them the road is now clear to the promised land." Of their commitment, Debs added, "These are Socialists, real Socialists, and they are ready for action, and if the time comes when men are needed at the front to fight and die for the cause the farmers of Texas and Oklahoma will be found there and their wives and children will not be far behind."[31] You don't build that kind of movement with policy one-pagers and polling data. It comes from the radical belief that a better world is possible, and the confidence that it will be built by the working class.

* * *

The idea of the cooperative commonwealth exists today. But nothing will change in Texas or anywhere else until the working class, those who produce society's wealth, get organized. Today, there is much debate about whether people should organize within the Democratic Party or work to launch an independent political party. There are plenty of lessons from Texas's radical history, but focusing on this question misses the point. Neither the People's Party nor the Socialist Party simply materialized after a convention. Neither could have existed without the work done by the Farmers' Alliance in politicizing those being crushed by the crop-lien system, or by the Knights of Labor, who built a class consciousness among workers and farmers that understood its needs would never be met by the ruling class. When those Texans gaveled in the birth of the People's Party, they were already representatives of a real, living, working-class movement, built on actual connections, shared perspective, and crucially, trust. When delegates spoke of "the people," those in attendance knew exactly who "the people" were, and weren't. In other words, to have a People's Party, you need to have people. Today, that means organizing people into the labor movement, or renters into tenants unions. It can take new forms as well. For example, Texans face a future of increased water shortages due to the pilfering of our natural resources by corporations. Imagine organizing everyday people into citizen councils to demand that their government—city, state, local, and national—ensures the preservation of our water systems.

We live in an increasingly anti-social era. We may share many of the economic conditions that Texas radicals have had in the past, but we are far less connected. We don't have an equivalent of the Farmers' Alliance today, nor the Renters' Union. Building this kind of class-rooted organization will be a necessary first step in reviving the Texas radical tradition. The encampments, the radical newspapers, the entire *social life* must be rebuilt. Digital organizing, both as forms of communication and through media, will be important, but an overreliance on platforms designed to distract and isolate must be avoided. Our new organizations will likely take various forms, but they must address the fundamental questions people are asking, and maintain a ruthless commitment to meeting their needs through profound change.

A strong set of political demands is important, but a key lesson from the success of the People's Party and Farmers' Alliance was identifying the cause of people's suffering. What is the crop-lien system of today? Who are the landlords, the cattle barons, the timber barons, of today?

Contrary to popular belief, Texas is not a conservative state. Conservatives have ruled the state for a long time, as both Democrats and Republicans, but there is a radical tradition with deep roots beneath the surface. The Right has done a great job of connecting the history of Texas to their vision, which they call "limited government"—a fancy way of saying government by and for the rich. There is no better example of this than the time of the Fence Cutters. When the government finally got involved, fence-cutting was made into a felony while the act of fencing off land to steal more property was decreed a misdemeanor. One set of rules for the elite, and another for us all. This kind of tradition has existed in Texas from the beginning. But there is another tradition, one committed to democracy and justice, that is just as present, but has been out of power for too long. Texans who want to fight for democracy, for the working class, and for the cooperative commonwealth should take pride in our radical history. As Thomas Hickey said to a crowd in Ellison Springs:

> "In this fight for universal freedom, I am confident that the old Lone Star State will take her place where the battle rages hardest and the call for men is heard. This has been our history in the past from the days of the Alamo to the close of the nineteenth century when the famous Populist delegates of 103 Texans stood like a stone wall against the fusion with Bryan and the donk that resulted in defeat and despair."

> "It was in Texas that the banner of the Farmers Union was first hoisted. It was in Texas that the Knights of Labor entered the farming regions while the other agricultural states stood back..."

> "I have no fear but that Texas will remain true to its revolutionary traditions and that in this great commonwealth, kissed by the Red River and washed by the Gulf where the sweet magnolia lends its fragrance to the southern air; in this favorite land of glorious sunshine we will take a leaf from the books of the life of our fathers, capture the citadel of privilege, overthrow landlordism, abolish rent, interest and profit,

make use and occupancy the title of the land, sit under our own vine and fig tree and thus by establishing industrial freedom among men we will have lived the life a man who has been true to his god, his country and humanity."[32]

A lot is made about Texas and free enterprise. About how it aligns with certain Texan values of resilience and individualism. For some, that is certainly true. But for others, those of the radical and deep-rooted Texan tradition, when the 'money-god" came to the Lone Star State, they did not bow down to this deity. No, they did not. They got out their clippers and they got to work cutting fences.

Epilogue

Fritz Tegener was born in Prussia in 1813. He came to Comfort, Texas, in 1854 to live among the Freidenker (Free Thinkers), an agnostic philosophical movement that advocated for reason over religiosity.[33] Germans like Tegener came to Texas to settle the Hill Country following the failed revolutions in Europe of 1848. Most were unaware that the land designated as their new home was not ideal for farming, or that its active border with Comancheria would make them a frequent target of raids. But these industrious and stubborn people made their homes amongst the limestone hills and cold-spring water, the most beautiful part of Texas. The landscape was the ideal home for radicals, its geographic independence allowing German Texans to live unbothered by the rest of Texas. The abolitionists, utopian socialists, and the Freidenker thrived until the Civil War, when the location of their settlements, just south of the Capitol in Austin, made them suspect to the Confederate government.

Texas's German population was largely anti-slavery and—like Sam Houston, the founder of Texas—loyal to the Union over the newly formed Confederacy. As violence increased against those with pro-Union sympathies and the prospect of conscription loomed, Tegener, along with approximately sixty others, attempted to flee. The German Texans had organized themselves into a militia to protect their "settlements against marauding Indians and outlaws."[34] Tegener had also helped organize another group, the Union Loyal League, which sought to prevent the conscription of Unionists into the Confederate army.[35] In August of 1862, 61 pro-Union Texans marched southwest from Turtle Creek, near Kerrville, on their way to Mexico.[36]

Confederate Captain James Duff, who was in the area to quell pro-Unionist activity, gave First Lieutenant Colin McRae command of 96 Confederates to pursue the fleeing Texans.[37] The Confederates pursued them for days before catching up to them on the banks of the Nueces River. The German Texans had spotted horsemen trailing their company, but Tegener was unbothered, and the company, camping in a rather exposed area under a "scattering of cedar trees," had only two men on watch.[38] Separating into two groups, the Confederates prepared to attack the sleeping German Texans, lying in wait until an excitable Texas Rebel fired his rifle, killing one of the watchmen. The attack had begun.

The men under the command of Tegener fought bravely against the Confederates, despite their disadvantage in numbers and position. After repelling the first barrage, where two were killed and four were wounded—including Tegener, who had been shot twice—the German Texans fortified their position.[39] Unsure of just how outnumbered they were, but sure they were outnumbered, a handful of men fled the camp, leaving just "thirty or thirty-five unwounded defenders."[40]

The men continued to defend their position, goading the Confederates into attacking. One Confederate who charged at the makeshift barricade was subsequently shot in the head, and McRae himself was shot twice.[41] Despite the Confederates' superior numbers and arms, the tenacity of the German Texans momentarily drove the Confederates back. With Tegener and many others wounded, Emil Schreiner yelled, "laszt uns unser Leben so teuer wie moglich verkaufen (Let us sell our lives as dearly as we can)."[42] The German Texans fought hard, but the Confederates were soon able to take the camp. Tegener and five other men escaped, but the other Union defenders were not so lucky.[43] Dishonorably, McRae's men took "nine to eleven wounded" captives, marched them into the trees, and murdered them.[44] The bodies of the brave defenders were left to rot under the Texas sun.

The bloody Nueces Massacre inspired Texans to find ways to fight back and avoid the draft, a draft from which wealthy slaveholders were exempted. Some opponents of the war took drastic steps—cutting off their fingers, and in at least one extreme case, suicide.[45] The Confederates continued to chase those who fled, and more German Texans were executed. But others lived. Fritz Tegener went to Mexico and spent the war working as a gold miner. Upon his return, he played an active role in politics, serving in the Texas House of Representatives during Reconstruction.[46]

* * *

Today in Comfort, Texas, there stands a monument, Treue der Union Monument, where the recoverable bodies were buried in 1865. One of the few monuments to the Union in the South, and among the earliest erected, it's a testament to the brave sacrifice these men made, and a reminder of Texas's infernal contradictions. Calling this event the "Battle of the Nueces" or the "Nueces Massacre" will put you on one side or another of a conflict that is over 150 years old. Which one is the "real" Texas? Colin McRae was born in Texas, but he was under the command of Scottish-born James Duff, who arrived in the U.S. just five years before Fritz Tegener settled in Comfort. There is a Texas-sized thread stretching from the Alamo to the Populists, the Socialists to the Brotherhood of the Timber Workers, and to the brave Union men standing on the banks of the Nueces. It stretches to all of those who take on impossible odds, stay true to their principles, and fight.

Notes

Introduction - Can We Take Hold Of Our History?

1. Marjory Harper. "Emigrant Strikebreakers: Scottish Granite Cutters and the Texas Capitol Boycott." *The Southwestern Historical Quarterly* 95, no. 4 (1992): 483. http://www.jstor.org/stable/30242001.

2. Justin Miller. "Beto Tried to Win a Texas That Doesn't Quite Exist Yet." The *Texas Observer*. November 7, 2018. https://www.texasobserver.org/beto-tried-to-win-a-texas-that-doesnt-quite-exist-yet/.

3. Sean Collins Walsh. "Congressman Beto O'Rourke: Trump's wall is 'racist'." *Austin-American Statesman* January 26, 2017 https://www.statesman.com/story/news/2017/01/27/congressman-beto-orourke-trumps-wall-is-racist/10415933007/

4. Beto O'Rourke, "Watch Beto's Full Concession Speech," *Washington Post*, November 7, 2018 https://www.washingtonpost.com/video/politics/watch-beto-orourkes-full-concession-speech/2018/11/07/56550e12-e253-11e8-ba30-a7ded04d8fac_video.html Colin Allred, "Colin Allred concedes: FULL SPEECH" *Fox 4 Dallas Fort Worth*, Youtube, November 5, 2024 https://www.youtube.com/watch?v=3kMS4ACXUkU

5. Astudillo, Carla. "Fundraising in Ted Cruz and Colin Allred's U.S. Senate Race." The Texas Tribune, The Texas Tribune, 18 July 2024, www.texastribune.org/2024/07/18/ted-cruz-colin-allred-fundraising-2024/.

6. Phillip Bump. "Texans Preferred O'Rourke to Cruz — At Least, Texans Born in Texas Did." *Washington Post*, November 9, 2018.

https://www.washingtonpost.com/politics/2018/11/09/texans-preferred-orourke-cruz-least-texans-born-texas-did/ and "Exit Polls." *CNN*, November 6, 2018. https://www.cnn.com/election/2018/exit-polls/texas/senate.

7. For more on this see: James Gimpel & Daron Shaw, "Long Distance Migration as a Two-Step Sorting Process: The Resettlement of Californians in Texas," *Political Behavior*. https://doi.org/10.1007/s11109-023-09898-3

8. "Texas Population by Year, County, Race, & More." *USAFacts*, June 11, 2025. https://usafacts.org/data/topics/people-society/population-and-demographics/our-changing-population/state/texas/?endDate=2022-01-01&startDate=1970-01-01.

9. United States Census Bureau. "State-level Urban and Rural Information for the 2020 Census and 2010 Census" *Urban and Rural*. 2024. https://www.census.gov/programs-surveys/geography/guidance/geo-areas/urban-rural.html

10. Anastasia Goodwin and Libby Seline, "Houston poverty rates the highest among major U.S. metros, new Census data shows," *Houston Chronicle*, September 14, 2023, https://www.houstonchronicle.com/news/houston-texas/census/article/houston-poverty-rate-increase-18365435.php

11. Sofia Calderon, "Texas Poverty Data Brief 2025," *Every Texan*, March 11, 2025 https://storymaps.arcgis.com/stories/d452c0bd12e648879b853161a836a713

12. U.S. Census Bureau, "Income in the Past 12 Months (in 2024 Inflation-Adjusted Dollars)," American Community Survey, ACS 1-Year Estimates Subject Tables, Table S1901, accessed on November 25, 2025, https://data.census.gov/table/ACSST1Y2024.S1901?g=010XX00US$0400000_040XX00US06,48_160XX00US0263170.

13. W. L. Garvin and S. O. Daws, *History of the National Farmers' Alliance and Co-Operative Union of America* (Jacksboro, Tex.:

J. N. Rogers & Co., 1887), p. VIII, PDF, https://www.loc.gov/item/09000479/.

14. Ross Ramsey, "UT/TT Poll: Majority of Texans Oppose Permitless Carry, Would Ban Police Chokeholds and Taxpayer-funded Lobbying." *Texas Tribune*, May 3, 2021. https://www.texastribune.org/2021/05/03/texas-voters-legislature-poll/.

15. Brennan Gardner Rivas,. "An Unequal Right to Bear Arms: State Weapons Laws and White Supremacy in Texas, 1836–1900." *The Southwestern Historical Quarterly* 121, no. 3 (2018): 284–303. http://www.jstor.org/stable/44648385.

16. Kayla Guo and Alejandro Serrano. "Dan Patrick Calls for Resignation of Alamo Trust President over Views on How the Alamo's History Should Be Told." The Texas Tribune. October 23, 2025. https://www.texastribune.org/2025/10/23/texas-alamo-trust-dan-patrick-dissertation-history-politics-2/.

17. Harvey J. Kaye, "The Year FDR Sought to Make America 'Fairly Radical,'" *BillMoyers.com*, June 20, 2016, https://billmoyers.com/story/year-fdr-sought-make-america-fairly-radical/.

Part I: The Birth of Populism

1. John L. McCarty, *Maverick Town: The Story of Old Tascosa* (University of Oklahoma Press, 1988), 108.

2. McCarty, *Maverick Town*, 111.

3. McCarty, *Maverick Town*, 111.

4. Mark Lause, *The Great Cowboy Strike: Bullets, Ballots, and Class Conflicts in the American West* (Verso Books, 2018), 90.

5. Mark Lause, *The Great Cowboy Strike*, 91.

6. Donald F. Schofield, "Lee, William McDole," *Handbook of Texas Online*, accessed May 12, 2025, https://www.tshaonline.org/handbook/entries/lee-william-mcdole.

7. McCarty, *Maverick Town*, 111.

NOTES

8.   McCarty, *Maverick Town*, 111.

9.   Lause, *The Great Cowboy Strike*, 95.

10.   Lause, 94.

11.   Lause, *The Great Cowboy Strike*, 100.

12.   Robert E. Zeigler, "Cowboy Strike of 1883," *Handbook of Texas Online*, accessed May 12, 2025, https://www.tshaonline.org/handbook/entries/cowboy-strike-of-1883.

13.   Robert E. Zeigler, "Cowboy Strike of 1883," *Handbook of Texas Online*, accessed January 16, 2025, https://www.tshaonline.org/handbook/entries/cowboy-strike-of-1883.

14.   Clay Coppedge, "Revolt On The Range," *Texas Co-op Power*, March 2014, https://texascooppower.com/revolt-on-the-range/

15.   "Heritage of Texas Labor," *Texas AFL-CIO* https://texasaflcio.org/heritage-texas-labor

16.   Lause, *The Great Cowboy Strike*, 103; *Third Annual Report of the Commissioner of Labor, 1887: Strikes and Lockouts* (Washington: Government Printing Office, 1888), 580–583. https://fraser.stlouisfed.org/title/6306/item/608431, accessed on November 25, 2025.

17.   Lause, *The Great Cowboy Strike*, 92.

18.   Lause, *The Great Cowboy Strike*, 104.

19.   Dulcie Sullivan, *The LS Brand: The Story Of A Texas Panhandle Ranch*, (University of Texas Press, 1968), 67.

20.   Lause, *The Great Cowboy Strike*, 106.

21.   Lause, 110.

22.   Lause, 110.

23.   Sullivan, *The LS Brand*, 87-88.

24.   Leon C. Metz, *Patt Garrett: The Story of a Western Lawman* (University of Oklahoma Press, 1983), 141.

25.   Metz, *Pat Garrett*, 142.

26.   Lause,111; Metz, 142.

27.   Metz, 145.

28. Metz, 144.

29. Metz, 145; Lause, 112.

30. Sullivan, *LS Brand*, 67.

31. William H. Hutchinson, "The Cowboy and the Class Struggle (Or, Never Put Marx in the Saddle)," *Arizona and the West* 14, no. 4 (1972): 325, http://www.jstor.org/stable/40168107.

32. Hutchinson, "The Cowboy and the Class Struggle," 330.

33. David L. Wheeler, "The Blizzard of 1886 and Its Effect on the Range Cattle Industry in the Southern Plains." *The Southwestern Historical Quarterly* 94, no. 3 (1991): 427. http://www.jstor.org/stable/30238759.

34. Wheeler, "The Blizzard of 1886," 423.

35. Wayne Gard. "The Fence-Cutters." *The Southwestern Historical Quarterly* 51, no. 1 (1947): 1–15. http://www.jstor.org/stable/30236110.

36. Wayne Gard, "Fence Cutting," *Handbook of Texas Online*, accessed May 15, 2025, https://www.tshaonline.org/handbook/entries/fence-cutting.

37. Gard, "The Fence-Cutters," 3.

38. Gard, "The Fence-Cutters," 5.

39. Stephen Harrigan, *Big Wonderful Thing: A History of Texas*, (University of Texas Press, 2019), 365.

40. Hugh Allen Anderson, "XIT Ranch," *Handbook of Texas Online*, accessed May 15, 2025, https://www.tshaonline.org/handbook/entries/xit-ranch.

41. Gard, "The Fence-Cutters," 8.

42. Gard, "The Fence-Cutters," 8.

43. Gard, "The Fence-Cutters," 6.

44. Earl W. Hayter, "Barbed Wire Fencing: A Prairie Invention: Its Rise and Influence in the Western States." *Agricultural History* 13, no. 4 (1939): 204. http://www.jstor.org/stable/3739686.

45. *Fort Worth Daily Gazette.* (Fort Worth, Tex.), Vol. 8, No. 26, Ed. 1, Tuesday, January 29, 1884, newspaper, January 29, 1884; Fort Worth, Texas. (https://texashistory.unt.edu/ark:/67531/metapth85244/m1/2/: accessed May 16, 2025), University of North Texas Libraries, The Portal to Texas History, https://texashistory.unt.edu;.

46. Wayne Gard, "Fence Cutting," *Handbook of Texas Online,* accessed May 16, 2025, https://www.tshaonline.org/handbook/entries/fence-cutting.

47. *Fort Worth Daily Gazette,* January 29, 1884.

48. Gard, "The Fence-Cutters," 11.

49. Gard, "The Fence-Cutters," 11.

50. Gard, "The Fence-Cutters," 12.

51. Gard, "The Fence-Cutters," 9.

52. Hugh Allen Anderson, "Big Die-Up," *Handbook of Texas Online,* accessed May 16, 2025, https://www.tshaonline.org/handbook/entries/big-die-up.

53. Wheeler, "The Blizzard of 1886," 430-431.

54. *The Galveston Daily News.* (Galveston, Tex.), Vol. 42, No. 260, Ed. 1 Friday, December 7, 1883, newspaper, December 7, 1883; Galveston, Texas. (https://texashistory.unt.edu/ark:/67531/metapth464621/m1/2/: accessed May 16, 2025), University of North Texas Libraries, The Portal to Texas History, https://texashistory.unt.edu; crediting Abilene Library Consortium.

55. *The Galveston Daily News,* December 7, 1883.

56. Lawrence Goodwyn, *The Populist Moment: A Short History of the Agrarian Revolt in America* (Oxford University Press, 1978), 25.

57. C. Vann Woodward, *Origins of the New South, 1877–1913* (Louisiana State University Press, 1951), 108.

58. Edward King, James Wells Champney, and Jay I. Kislak Collection, *The Great South: A Record of Journeys in Louisiana,*

Texas, the Indian Territory, Missouri, Arkansas, Mississippi, Alabama, Georgia, Florida, South Carolina, North Carolina, Kentucky, Tennessee, Virginia, West Virginia, and Maryland (American Publishing Company, 1875), 775. PDF, https://www.loc.gov/item/rc01002442/.

59. Ralph Smith, "The Farmer's Alliance in Texas, 1875–1900: A Revolt against Bourbon and Bourgeois Democracy," *The Southwestern Historical Quarterly* 48, no. 3 (1945): 347, http://www.jstor.org/stable/30236077.

60. Goodwyn, *The Populist Moment*, 22.

61. Goodwyn, *The Populist Moment*, 22.

62. Goodwyn, *The Populist Moment*, 22.

63. James R. Green, *Grass-Roots Socialism: Radical Movements in the Southwest 1895-1943* (Louisana State University Press, 1978), 70-72.

64. James L. Haley, *Passionate Nation: The Epic History of Texas* (New York: Free Press, 2009), 384–386.

65. Haley, *Passionate Nation: The Epic History of Texas,* 386.

66. Roger A. Griffin, "Land Grants for Internal Improvements," *Handbook of Texas Online*, accessed February 14, 2025, https://www.tshaonline.org/handbook/entries/land-grants-for-internal-improvements.

67. Donna A. Barnes, "Farmers' Alliance," *Handbook of Texas Online*, accessed May 18, 2025, https://www.tshaonline.org/handbook/entries/farmers-alliance.

68. Milton Park, *The Southern Mercury* (Dallas, Tex.), Vol. 11, No. 46, Ed. 1, November 17, 1892, accessed February 18, 2025, https://texashistory.unt.edu/ark:/67531/metapth185491/.

69. Donna Barnes, *Farmers in Rebellion* (Austin, TX: University of Texas Press, 1984), 55.

70. Barnes, *Farmers in Rebellion,* 55.

71. Donna A. Barnes, "Farmers' Alliance," *Handbook of Texas Online*, accessed May 18, 2025, https://www.tshaonline.org/handbook/entries/farmers-alliance.

72. Donna A. Barnes, "Farmers' Alliance," *Handbook of Texas Online*, accessed May 18, 2025, https://www.tshaonline.org/handbook/entries/farmers-alliance.

73. Barnes, *Farmers in Rebellion*, 61.

74. Barnes, *Farmers in Rebellion*, 61-62.

75. Barnes, *Farmers in Rebellion*, 62.

76. Barnes, *Farmers in Rebellion*, 63.

77. Goodwyn, *The Populist Moment*, 26.

78. W. L. Garvin and S. O. Daws, History of the National farmers' alliance and co-operative union of America (Jacksboro, Tex.: J. N. Rogers & Co., 1887), p. VIII, PDF, https://www.loc.gov/item/09000479/. https://www.loc.gov/item/09000479/.

79. Barnes, *Farmers in Rebellion*, 53.

80. Ralph Smith, "The Farmer's Alliance in Texas, 1875-1900: A Revolt against Bourbon and Bourgeois Democracy," *The Southwestern Historical Quarterly* 48, no. 3 (1945): 365. http://www.jstor.org/stable/30236077.

81. Goodwyn, *The Populist Moment*, 117.

82. Goodwyn, 117.

83. *Fort Worth Gazette* (Fort Worth, Tex.), Vol. 15, No. 286, Ed. 1, Tuesday, July 28, 1891, newspaper, July 28, 1891; Fort Worth, Texas, University of North Texas Libraries, The Portal to Texas History, https://texashistory.unt.edu/ark:/67531/metapth89756/m1/1/, accessed March 6, 2025, as cited by Donna A. Barnes, *Farmers in Rebellion*, 124.

84. Barnes, 125.

85. Goodwyn, *The Populist Moment*, 33.

86. Goodwyn, 33.

87. Barnes, *Farmers in Rebellion*, 68.

88. C.L.R. James, "Every Cook Can Govern," *Marxists.org,* original. *Correspondence*, Vol. 2, No. 12. June 1956. https://www. marxists.org/archive/james-clr/works/1956/06/every-cook.htm.

89. George N Green. "The Texas Labor Movement, 1870-1920." *The Southwestern Historical Quarterly* 108, no. 1 (2004): 4. http://www.jstor.org/stable/30239492.

90. W. R. Lamb, as quoted by Goodwyn, *The Populist Moment*, 38.

91. Goodwyn, *The Populist Moment*, 38.

92. Goodwyn, 39.

93. Goodwyn, 37.

94. Goodwyn, 37.

95. George N. Green, "The Texas Labor Movement," *Southwest Historical Quarterly* 2004, 4.

96. Ernest William Winkler, ed., *Platforms of Political Parties in Texas* (University of Texas Press, September 20, 1916), 235.

97. Winkler, *Platforms of Political Parties in Texas*, 235.

98. Goodwyn, *The Populist Moment*, 42.

99. C. Vann Woodward, *Origins of the New South, 1877–1913* (Baton Rouge: Louisiana State University Press, 1951), 190.

100. Robert C. McMath Jr., *Populist Vanguard: A History of The Southern Farmers' Alliance* (The University of North Carolina Press, 1975), 90.

101. McMath, *Populist Vanguard,* 90.

102. Gregg Cantrell, *The People's Revolt* (New Haven, CT: Yale University Press, 2020),129-130.

103. Cantrell, *The People's Revolt*, 130-131.

104. Milton Park, *The Southern Mercury* (Dallas, Tex.), Vol. 11, No. 18, Ed. 1, Thursday, May 5, 1892, newspaper, May 5, 1892; Dallas, Texas, University of North Texas Libraries, The Portal to Texas History, https://texashistory.unt.edu/ark:/67531/ metapth185463/, accessed March 4, 2025.

105. Milton Park, *The Southern Mercury* (Dallas, Tex.), Vol. 10, No. 23, Ed. 1, Thursday, June 4, 1891, newspaper, June 4, 1891; Dallas, Texas, University of North Texas Libraries, The Portal to Texas History, https://texashistory.unt.edu/ark:/67531/metapth185416/, accessed March 4, 2025.

106. Park, *The Southern Mercury*, June 4, 1891.

107. As quoted in: Harrigan, *Big Wonderful Thing*, 332

108. Woodward, *Origins of the New South*, 204.

109. C. W. Raines, Ed. *Speeches and State Papers of James Stephen Hogg, Ex-Governor of Texas, With a Sketch of His Life*; (The State Printing Company, 1905), 39, https://texashistory.unt.edu/ark:/67531/metapth29400/m1/41/: accessed September 24, 2025, University of North Texas Libraries, The Portal to Texas History, https://texashistory.unt.edu.

110. As cited in Matthew Hild's excellent article on the role of the Knights of Labor in the Third Party movement in Texas. Matthew Hild. "The Knights of Labor and the Third-Party Movement in Texas, 1886–1896." *The Southwestern Historical Quarterly* 119, no. 1 (2015): 35. http://www.jstor.org/stable/24388910.

111. Goodwyn, *Populist Moment*, 149.

112. Barnes, *Farmers in Rebellion*, 118.

113. Barnes, 119.

114. Roscoe Martin, *The People's Party in Texas* (Austin: University of Texas Press, 1933), 25.

115. Woodward, *Origins of the New South*, 238.

116. Ralph Smith, "The Farmer's Alliance in Texas, 1875-1900: A Revolt against Bourbon and Bourgeois Democracy," *The Southwestern Historical Quarterly* 48, no. 3 (1945): 365, http://www.jstor.org/stable/30236077.

117. Martin, *The People's Party in Texas*, 37.

118. Martin, *The People's Party in Texas*, 36.

119. Martin, 37.

120. Woodward, *Origins of the New South*, 238.

121. Martin, *The People's Party in Texas*, 38.

122. Milton Park, *The Southern Mercury* (Dallas, Tex.), Vol. 10, No. 29, Ed. 1, Thursday, July 16, 1891, newspaper, July 16, 1891; Dallas, Texas, University of North Texas Libraries, The Portal to Texas History, https://texashistory.unt.edu/ark:/67531/metapth185421/m1/9/, accessed March 7, 2025.

123. Hild. "The Knights of Labor and the Third-Party Movement in Texas," 37.

124. Winkler, *Platforms of Political Parties in Texas*, 295.

125. Winkler, 293.

126. Winkler, 294.

127. Winkler, 295.

128. Winkler, 297.

129. Thomas Alter II. *Toward a Cooperative Commonwealth: The Transplanted Roots of Farmer-Labor Radicalism in Texas.* (University of Illinois Press, 2022), 84–85; Martin, *The People's Party in Texas*, 42–43; Winkler, *Platforms of Political Parties in Texas*, 300–301.

130. Wayne Alvord, "T. L. Nugent, Texas Populist," *The Southwestern Historical Quarterly* 57, no. 1 (1953): 67, http://www.jstor.org/stable/30237644.

131. This description is based on Roscoe Martin's background on the populist leader 115-118

132. For an excellent investigation into Nugent's religious beliefs see Wayne Alvord. "T. L. Nugent, Texas Populist." *The Southwestern Historical Quarterly* 57, no. 1 (1953): 75. http://www.jstor.org/stable/30237644.

133. Goodwyn, *The Populist Moment*, 191–192; Alvord, 71.

134. Meagan Day, "There Once Was A Socialist College In The Rural South," *Jacobin*, June 14, 2021, https://jacobin.com/2021/06/

commonwealth-college-arkansas-socialist-education-debs-communist-party.

135. Thomas Nugent, as quoted in, *The Southern Mercury* (Dallas, Tex.), August 30, 1894. Also cited in Wayne Alvord, "T. L. Nugent, Texas Populist," 79.

136. Karl Marx, *The Marx-Engels Reader,* ed. Robert C. Tucker,(W. W. Norton, 1972), 476.

137. Goodwyn, *The Populist Moment,* 190.

138. Alter II, *Toward a Cooperative Commonwealth,* 90.

139. Worth Robert Miller and Stacy G. Ulbig, "Building a Populist Coalition in Texas, 1892–1896," *The Journal of Southern History* 74, no. 2 (2008): 263. http://www.jstor.org/stable/27650143.

140. Woodward,. *Origins of the New South,* 261.

141. Barnes, *Farmers in Rebellion,* 142.

142. Alter II, 90; see also Martin, 210; and Barnes, 142.

143. Roscoe, 210.; Miller and Ulbig, 265.

144. Miller and Ulbig, 265.

145. Hild, 39.

146. Martin, 173.

147. Miller & Ulbig, 267.

148. Miller & Ulbig, 267; and Goodwyn, 192.

149. Woodward, 254; Goodwyn, 119.

150. Goodwyn, 119.

151. Jack Abramowitz, "The Negro in the Agrarian Revolt," *Agricultural History* 24, no. 2 (1950): 89–95. http://www.jstor.org/stable/3741057. Citing Ernest W. Winkler, *Platforms of Political Parties in Texas* (Austin: University of Texas Press, 1916), 187.

152. Woodward, 255.

153. As quoted by Woodward, 220.

154. Woodward, 192.

155. Goodwyn, 123.

156. Goodwyn, 120; William F. Holmes, "Colored Farmers' Alliance," *Handbook of Texas Online*, accessed March 20, 2025, https://www.tshaonline.org/handbook/entries/colored-farmers-alliance.

157. Goodwyn, 119; Woodward, 119.

158. Goodwyn, 146; Cantrell, The *People's Revolt,* 58.

159. Carl H. Moneyhon, "Republican Party," *Handbook of Texas Online*, accessed March 20, 2025, https://www.tshaonline.org/handbook/entries/republican-party.

160. Alter II, 6.

161. Paul D. Casdorph, "Lily-White Movement," *Handbook of Texas Online*, accessed March 20, 2025, https://www.tshaonline.org/handbook/entries/lily-white-movement.

162. Woodward, 219.

163. Woodward, 219.

164. Cantrell, *The People's Revolt*, 186.

165. *Dallas Morning News*, August 18, 1891, as quoted in Woodward, 256.

166. *Dallas Morning News*, August 18, 1891, as quoted in Woodward, 256.

167. Woodward, 256; Martin, 94.

168. Goodwyn, 193.

169. Martin, 126; and Jack Abramowitz, "John B. Rayner—A Grass-Roots Leader," *The Journal of Negro History* 36, no. 2 (1951): 162. https://doi.org/10.2307/2715417.

170. Martin, 126.

171. *Southern Mercury*, June 13, 1895.

172. Goodwyn, 193.

173. Milton Park, *The Southern Mercury* (Dallas, Tex.), Vol. 16, No. 25, June 24, 1897, p. 8.

174. Cantrell, *The People's Revolt*, 189.

175. Woodward, 256.

176. Cantrell, 190; Woodward, 256.

177. Cantrell, 190.

178. Park, *Southern Mercury*, Vol. 13, No. 46, November 15, 1894, p. 5, https://texashistory.unt.edu/ark:/67531/metapth185587/m1/4/.

179. *Southern Mercury*, November 15, 1894, 4.

180. *Southern Mercury*, Vol. 13, No. 49, December 6, 1894, 13.

181. Southern Mercury, Vol. 13, No. 49, December 6, 1894, 13.

182. Southern Mercury, Vol. 13, No. 49, December 6, 1894, 13.

183. Barnes, 154.

184. Woodward, 274.

185. Martin, 170.

186. Martin, 171-172.

187. Woodward, 264.

188. Hild, 40.

189. *Southern Mercury*, Vol. 13, No. 32, August 16, 1894, p. 10,

190. Miller and Ulbig, 283.

191. Governor Hogg of Texas was vocally critical of Cleveland's decision, not necessarily in support of labor, but saw the attack against ARU as "a fatal blow at State's rights," and said that he would oppose Federal troops entering Texas to break a strike. Woodward, 268-269. For more on the correlation between Knights of Labor and populism see Miller and Ulbig, 255–96.

192. Barnes, 158.

193. Barnes, 159.

194. Barnes, 157–158.

195. Barnes, 158–159.

196. Woodward, 282.

197. Martin, 239.

198. Barnes, 178-179.

199. Cantrell, 355.

200. Alter, 103; Barnes, 178.

201. Cantrell, 347.

202. *Southern Mercury*, Vol. 15, No. 34, August 20, 1896, 14.

203. Barnes, 164-165.

204. Woodward, 287.

205. Robert Worth Miller, "Building a Progressive Coalition in Texas: The Populist-Reform Democrat Rapprochement, 1900-1907." *The Journal of Southern History* 52, no. 2 (1986): 165.

206. Cantrell, 387.

207. Cantrell, 388.

208. Miller, "Building a Progressive Coalition in Texas," 165.

209. Goodwyn, 324.

210. T. A. Hickey, *The Rebel* (Hallettsville, Tex.), Vol. [5], No. 224, November 6, 1915, https://texashistory.unt.edu/ark:/67531/metapth394547/m1/1

211. Goodwyn, 327.

212. Goodwyn, 326-327.

213. James R. Green, 2.

Part 2: Let Us Arise

1. Peter H. Buckingham, *"Red Tom" Hickey: The Uncrowned King of Texas Socialism* (Texas A&M University Press, 2020), 272; Thomas A. Hickey, *The Rebel* (Hallettsville, Tex.), vol. 6, no. 304, ed. 1, June 2, 1917, newspaper, University of North Texas Libraries, The Portal to Texas History, https://texashistory.unt.edu/ark:/67531/metapth394758/m1/1/ (accessed March 31, 2025), crediting UT San Antonio Libraries Special Collections.

2. James R. Green, *Grass-Roots Socialism*, 71.

3. Benjamin H. Hibbard, "Tenancy in the Southern States," *The Quarterly Journal of Economics* 27, no. 3 (1913): 486, https://doi.org/10.2307/1883374.

4. Hibbard, "Tenancy in the Southern States," 20-21.

5. Eugene V. Debs, "Revolutionary Encampments," *National Rip-Saw* (St. Louis), September 1914, 12, https://www.marxists.org/history/usa/pubs/national-ripsaw/140900-nationalripsaw-v11n07w127.pdf. & Green, 153.

6. Robert Worth Miller. "Building a Progressive Coalition in Texas: The Populist-Reform Democrat Rapprochement, 1900-1907." The Journal of Southern History 52, no. 2 (1986): 164–66. & Alter, 112.

7. Alter, 112.

8. Miller, 174.

9. Miller, 174.

10. Miller, 174.

11. Green, 26.

12. Lawrence C. Goodwyn, "Populist Dreams and Negro Rights: East Texas as a Case Study." *The American Historical Review* 76, no. 5 (1971): 1437. https://doi.org/10.2307/1870515.

13. *The Daily Examiner*. (Navasota, Tex.), Vol. 5, No. 52, Ed. 1 Saturday, January 6, 1900, newspaper, January 6, 1900; Navasota, Texas. (https://texashistory.unt.edu/ark:/67531/metapth1336170/m1/2/: accessed October 16, 2025), University of North Texas Libraries, The Portal to Texas History, https://texashistory.unt.edu; crediting Navasota Public Library.

14. Goodwyn, "Populist Dreams," 1440.

15. Goodwyn, "Populist Dreams," 1440.

16. Goodwyn, "Populist Dreams," 1440.

17. Goodwyn, "Populist Dreams," 1443.

18. Goodwyn, "Populist Dreams," 1442.

19. Goodwyn, "Populist Dreams," 1443 - 1445.

20. Green, 308.

21. Green, 20.

22. "Eugene V. Debs," *AFL-CIO*, https://aflcio.org/about/history/labor-history-people/eugene-debs

23. Matthew Hild. "The Knights of Labor and the Third-Party Movement in Texas, 1886–1896." The Southwestern Historical Quarterly 119, no. 1 (2015): 43. http://www.jstor.org/stable/24388910.

24. Green, 20.

25. As hailed by his socialist contemporary and friend Covington Hall, who wrote Tom Hickey was the "uncrowned king of Texas socialism, but its despot and 'pop' as we." Peter Buckingham uses this as his title in his great biography of the Texas socialist. *"Red Tom" Tom Hickey The Uncrowned King of Texas Socialism* is a must read for anyone interested in Thomas Hickey or in American socialism more broadly.

26. Buckingham, 57.

27. Green, 20, 117.

28. Buckingham, 114-116.

29. H.L. Mitchell, one of the founders of the Southern Tenant Farmers' Union, has an incredible autobiography where he outlines the uniqueness of the Southern agrarian situation and outlines in detail the ways Midwestern and Northern Socialists failed to recognize this contradiction.

30. Karl Kautsky, "Socialist Agitation Among Farmers in America," *International Socialist Review*, Vol.3 (September 1902), pp.148-160. Via https://www.marxists.org/archive/kautsky/1902/09/farmers.htm.

31. Green, 39.

32. Goodwyn, *The Populist Moment*, 324.

33. *The Appeal to Reason*, January 18, 1902, https://www.marxists.org/history/usa/pubs/appeal-to-reason/020118-appealtoreason-w320.pdf.

34. Alter, 98; Green, 17-19, 141.

35. Green, 142.

36. Green, 143.

37. Green, 143.

38. Thomas A. Hickey, *The Rebel* (Hallettsville, Tex.), vol. 1, no. 1, ed. 1, July 1, 1911, newspaper, University of North Texas Libraries, The Portal to Texas History, https://texashistory.unt.edu/ark:/67531/metapth394574/m1/1/

39. *The Rebel*, July 1, 1911.

40. Green, 156-157.

41. Green, 156-157.

42. Green, 156-157.

43. Green, 156-157.

44. Green, 155.

45. Debs, "Revolutionary Encampments," *National Rip-Saw*, September 1914, 12.

46. Debs, "Revolutionary Encampments," *National Rip-Saw*, 1914, 12.

47. *The Rebel*, September 9, 1911.

48. *The Rebel*, September 9, 1911.

49. Green, 171.

50. Green, 171.

51. Green, 171.

52. Green, 175.

53. *The Rebel*, February 21, 1914; & Green, 165.

54. Karl Marx and Friedrich Engels, *The Communist Manifesto*, 1848, https://www.marxists.org/archive/marx/works/1848/communist-manifesto/ch01.htm#007.

55. *The Rebel*, October 14, 1916.

56. Winkler, *Platforms of Political Parties In Texas*, 528.

57. Alter, 124.

58. Winkler, 529.

59. Winkler, 529.

60. Winkler, 528-529.

61. Winkler, 528.

62. Green, 120-121. Keith L. King, "Andrews, Reddin, Jr.," *Handbook of Texas Online*, https://www.tshaonline.org/handbook/entries/andrews-reddin-jr (accessed April 18, 2025).

63. *The Rebel*, September 7, 1912.

64. Green, 120; & Alter, 128-129.

65. Buckingham, 192.

66. Buckingham, 192.

67. Green, 121.

68. Winkler, 567.

69. *The Rebel*, July 1, 1911.

70. *The Rebel*, September 14, 1912

71. The three parties Debs is referencing are the Democratic, Republican, and Theodore Roosevelt's Progressive Party. *The Rebel*, September 14, 1912.

72. Green, 241.

73. Green, 248.

74. Green, 249.

75. Alter, 130.

76. Green, 317.

77. Green, 76.

78. Green, 317.

79. Alter, 127.

80. Green, 116.

81. Alter, 144.

82. Green, 306.

83. *The Rebel*, October 7, 1911.

84. *The Rebel*, October 7, 1911.

85. Alter, 118.

86. Green, 112.

87. Green, 113.

88. Green, 110.

89. Alter, 136.

90. Alter, 136.

91. Green, 105.

92. Eugene V. Debs, "The Negro In The Class Struggle," *International Socialist Review*, Vol. IV, No. 5. November 1903. https://www.marxists.org/archive/debs/works/1903/negro.htm

93. Cantrell, *The People's Revolt*, 190.

94. *The Rebel*, April 24, 1915.

95. George T. Morgan, "The Gospel of Wealth Goes South: John Henry Kirby and Labor's Struggle for Self-Determination, 1901-1916." *The Southwestern Historical Quarterly* 75, no. 2 (1971): 188. http://www.jstor.org/stable/30236713.

96. Morgan, "The Gospel of Wealth Goes South," 170; James R. Green, "The Brotherhood of Timber Workers 1910-1913: A Radical Response To Industrial Capitalism In The Southern U.S.A.," *Past & Present*, Volume 60, Issue 1, August 1973, 170.

97. George T. Morgan, "The Gospel of Wealth Goes South," 188.

98. *The Rebel*, February 17, 1912.

99. Green, 204.

100. Green, 205.

101. George T. Morgan, Jr., "Kirby, John Henry," Handbook of Texas Online, accessed May 14, 2025, https://www.tshaonline.org/handbook/entries/kirby-john-henry.

102. Woodward, *Origins Of The New South*, 118.

103. James E. Fickle "'Comfortable and Happy'? Louisiana and Mississippi Lumber Workers, 1900-1950." *Louisiana History: The Journal of the Louisiana Historical Association* 40, no. 4 (1999): 423. http://www.jstor.org/stable/4233613.

104. Green, "Brotherhood Of Timber Workers," 167.

105. Green, "Brotherhood of Timber Workers," 164.

106. Green, "Brotherhood of Timber Workers," 164; & Green, *Grass-Roots Socialism*, 207.

107. Green, *Grass-Roots Socialism*, 207.

108. James C. Maroney, "Brotherhood of Timber Workers," Handbook of Texas Online, accessed May 14, 2025, https://www.tshaonline.org/handbook/entries/brotherhood-of-timber-workers.

109. Green, "Brotherhood of Timber Workers," 175.

110. Green, "Brotherhood of Timber Workers," 175.

111. William D. Haywood, "Timber Workers and Timbers Wolves," *International Socialist Review*, Vol. 13 No. 2, August 1912, pp. 105-110. Accessed https://www.marxists.org/history/usa/pubs/isr/v13n02-aug-1912-ISR-gog-ocr.pdf

112. James E. Fickle, "The Louisiana-Texas Lumber War of 1911-1912." *Louisiana History: The Journal of the Louisiana Historical Association* 16, no. 1 (1975): 64. http://www.jstor.org/stable/4231438.

113. Fickle, "The Louisiana-Texas Lumber War of 1911-1912." 63

114. Green, *Grassroots Socialism*, 210.

115. Fickle, "The Louisiana-Texas Lumber War of 1911-1912." 64.

116. James C. Maroney, "Brotherhood of Timber Workers," Handbook of Texas Online, accessed May 14, 2025, https://www.tshaonline.org/handbook/entries/brotherhood-of-timber-workers.

117. James C. Maroney, "Brotherhood of Timber Workers," Handbook of Texas Online, accessed May 14, 2025, https://www.tshaonline.org/handbook/entries/brotherhood-of-timber-workers.

118. Green, *Grassroots Socialism*, 209.

119. Green, *Brotherhood of Timber Workers*, 186. & Covington Hall, Edited by. David R. Roediger. *Labor Struggles in the Deep South & Other Writings*. (Charles H. Kerr Pub. Co, 1999.) 128.

There seems to be some disagreement about who said what; Covington Hall's account includes him joining Haywood in calling for the meeting to be joined together. After it was argued that having delegates sit separately should suffice to be in accordance with the law Hall and Haywood told those gathered if that if any attempts to arrest those in attendance are made, "all or none of us will go to jail, white and colored together."

120. Green, 211.

121. Green, 212.

122. Covington Hall, *Labor Struggles In The Deep South*, 129; Green, 210.

123. Green, "Brotherhood of Timber Workers," 164.

124. Covington Hall, *Labor Struggles In The Deep South*, 129.

125. *The Rebel*, October 7, 1911.

126. Morgan, "The Gospel of Wealth Goes South," 195.

127. Morgan, 193.

128. Green, "Brotherhood of Timber Workers," 194.

129. Green, "Brotherhood of Timber Workers," 187.

130. Green, "Brotherhood of Timber Workers," 180.

131. Green, "Brotherhood of Timber Workers," 181.

132. Green, "Brotherhood of Timber Workers," 181.

133. Green, "Brotherhood of Timber Workers," 198.

134. H.L. Mitchell, *Mean Things Happening In This Land: The Life and Times of H.L. Mitchell, Co-founder of the Southern Tenant Farmers Union* (Oklahoma University Press, 2008), 31.

135. Green, "Brotherhood of Timber Workers," 187.

136. Green, 266, 386.

137. James R. Green, "Tenant Farmer Discontent and Socialist Protest in Texas, 1901-1917." *The Southwestern Historical Quarterly* 81, no. 2 (1977): 141. http://www.jstor.org/stable/30238515.

138. *The Rebel*, September 28, 1912.

139. Alter, 137.

140. Alter, 160.

141. *The Rebel*, January 11, 1913.

142. *The Rebel,* May 3, 1913.

143. *The Rebel*, November 15, 1913; & November 20, 1915.

144. *The Rebel* September 27, 1913, & Alter, 150.

145. Green, 232.

146. *The Rebel,* September 20, 1913.

147. *The Rebel,* September 20, 1913.

148. Alter, 148.

149. *The Rebel* January 3, 1914.

150. *The Rebel* January 3, 1914.

151. Alter, 148.

152. *The Rebel*, November 28, 1914.

153. Stefan Cavazos, "Mártires de Texas," *Handbook of Texas Online*, accessed May 06, 2025, https://www.tshaonline.org/handbook/ entries/martires-de-texas.

154. Stefan Cavazos, "Mártires de Texas," *Handbook of Texas Online*

155. Stefan Cavazos, "Mártires de Texas," *Handbook of Texas Online*

156. Stefan Cavazos, "Mártires de Texas," *Handbook of Texas Online*

157. Covington Hall, *The Voice Of The People*, July 7 1914. accessed: https://www.marxists.org/history/usa/pubs/lumberjack/140707-voiceofthepeople-v3n27w078.pdf

158. *The Rebel*, February 20, 1915.

159. Stefan Cavazos, "Mártires de Texas," Handbook of Texas Online, accessed May 06, 2025, https://www.tshaonline.org/handbook/ entries/martires-de-texas.

160. Alter, 140.

161. Winkler, 591.

162. Patrick L. Cox, "'An Enemy Closer to Us than Any European Power': The Impact of Mexico on Texan Public Opinion before

World War I." *The Southwestern Historical Quarterly* 105, no. 1 (2001): 40–80. http://www.jstor.org/stable/30240307.

163. *The Rebel,* February 10, 1917.

164. *The Rebel,* February 10, 1917.

165. Teresa Palomo Acosta, "Partido Liberal Mexicano," *Handbook of Texas Online*, accessed May 06, 2025, https://www.tshaonline.org/handbook/entries/partido-liberal-mexicano.

166. Covington Hall, "I am Here for Labor" *International Socialist Review*, September 1912, 226. https://www.marxists.org/history/usa/pubs/isr/v13n03-sep-1912-ISR-gog-ocr.pdf

167. Alter, 146-147.

168. Alter, 138.

169. Alter, 138.

170. Green, 310, footnote 92.

171. Don M. Coerver, "Plan of San Diego," *Handbook of Texas Online,* accessed May 07, 2025, https://www.tshaonline.org/handbook/entries/plan-of-san-diego.

172. *The Rebel,* November 6, 1915.

173. *The Rebel,* 9, 1915.

174. Alter, 168; and Buckingham, 263.

175. Alter, 169.

176. *The Rebel,* April 1, 1916; & April 29, 1916.

177. Buckingham, 268.

178. Alter, 110.

179. Harrigan, *Big Wonderful Thing: A History of Texas,* 488.

180. Ralph W. Steen, "Ferguson, James Edward," *Handbook of Texas Online,* accessed May 08, 2025, https://www.tshaonline.org/handbook/entries/ferguson-james-edward.

181. Winkler, 608; Green, 296.

182. Buckingham, 229.

183. Winkler, 648.

184. Ralph W. Steen, "Ferguson, James Edward," *Handbook of Texas Online*, accessed May 08, 2025, https://www.tshaonline.org/handbook/entries/ferguson-james-edward.

185. Buckingham, 229.

186. Green, 299.

187. *The Rebel,* November 28, 1914.

188. *The Rebel,* November 28, 1914.

189. Green, 350.

190. Allan L. Benson, "What's Wrong with the Socialist Party," *The New Appeal*, (June 15, 1918) http://www.marxisthistory.org/history/usa/parties/spusa/1918/0615-benson-whatswrongwithspa.pdf

191. Green, 348; Buckingham, 279.

192. *The Rebel* November 11, 1916.

193. Green, 352.

194. Alter, 175.

195. Eugene V. Debs, "In Whose War Shall I Fight?," *Appeal to Reason,* September, 1915 as cited in https://www.marxists.org/history/etol/newspape/themilitant/socialist-appeal-1938/v02n14/debs.htm

196. *The Rebel,* May 26, 1917.

197. *The Rebel,* May 26, 1917.

198. Green, 173.

199. Alter, 182.

200. *The Rebel,* August 5, 1916.

201. Alter, 183.

202. Alter, 183.

203. Green, 355.

204. Alter, 183.

205. *The Rebel,* June 2, 1917.

206. Green, 356.

207. Buckingham, 278.

NOTES

Part 3: New Deal Blues

1. Harrigan, *Big Wonderful Thing: A History of Texas*, 227. & Jesús "Frank" de la Teja, "Seguin, Juan Nepomuceno," *Handbook of Texas Online*, accessed May 12, 2025, https://www.tshaonline.org/handbook/entries/seguin-juan-nepomuceno.

2. Emma Tenayuca, "Emma Tenayuca at 1985 IWD March." Museo Del Westside. Posted September 30, 2020. Video, https://www.youtube.com/watch?v=nZy5wv9_fnY.

3. Kenneth P Walker,. "The Pecan Shellers of San Antonio and Mechanization." *The Southwestern Historical Quarterly* 69, no. 1 (1965): 45. http://www.jstor.org/stable/30237885.

4. Walker, "The Pecan Shellers of San Antonio and Mechanization," 46.

5. "The Mexican Question in the Southwest," *The Communist* 18 (March 1939). 262-263. https://www.marxists.org/history/usa/pubs/communist/v18n03-mar-1939-The-Communist-OCR.pdf

6. Walker, "The Pecan Shellers of San Antonio and Mechanization," 47.

7. Walker, 45; & Richard Croxdale, "Pecan-Shellers' Strike," *Handbook of Texas Online*, accessed May 1, 2025, https://www.tshaonline.org/handbook/entries/pecan-shellers-strike.

8. Walker, 47.

9. Richard Croxdale, "Pecan-Shellers' Strike," *Handbook of Texas Online*, accessed May 2, 2025, https://www.tshaonline.org/handbook/entries/pecan-shellers-strike.

10. Geoffrey Rips. "Reporting On Pecan Workers In The '30's." The *Texas Observer*, October 28, 1983.

11. Billups, Robert S. "WAGES AND HOURS OF LABOR." *Monthly Labor Review* 44, no. 4 (1937): 940-41. http://www.jstor.org/stable/41815115.

12. Walker, 48.

13. Walker, 48.

14. Walker, 49.

15. Rips, the *Texas Observer*, October 28, 1983.

16. Richard Croxdale, "Pecan-Shellers' Strike," *Handbook of Texas Online*, accessed May 12, 2025, https://www.tshaonline.org/handbook/entries/pecan-shellers-strike.

17. R. Matt Abigail and Jazmin León, "Tenayuca, Emma Beatrice," *Handbook of Texas Online*, accessed May 12, 2025, https://www.tshaonline.org/handbook/entries/tenayuca-emma-beatrice.

18. Rips, the *Texas Observer*, October 28, 1983.

19. Vargas, Zaragosa. "Tejana Radical: Emma Tenayuca and the San Antonio Labor Movement during the Great Depression." *Pacific Historical Review* 66, no. 4 (1997): 554 & 558. https://doi.org/10.2307/3642237.

20. Rips, the *Texas Observer*, October 28, 1983.

21. R. Matt Abigail and Jazmin León, "Tenayuca, Emma Beatrice," *Handbook of Texas Online*, accessed May 12, 2025, https://www.tshaonline.org/handbook/entries/tenayuca-emma-beatrice.

22. Vargas, Zaragosa. "Tejana Radical: Emma Tenayuca and the San Antonio Labor Movement during the Great Depression." *Pacific Historical Review* 66, no. 4 (1997): 561

23. Rips, the *Texas Observer*, October 28, 1983.

24. R. Matt Abigail and Jazmin León, "Tenayuca, Emma Beatrice," *Handbook of Texas Online*, accessed May 12, 2025, https://www.tshaonline.org/handbook/entries/tenayuca-emma-beatrice.

25. Vargas, 566.

26. Walker, 50.

27. Walker, 51.

28. Walker, 52.

29. Walker. 51-52.

30. Rips, the *Texas Observer*, October 28, 1983.

31. Rips, the *Texas Observer*, October 28, 1983; R. Matt Abigail and Jazmin León, "Tenayuca, Emma Beatrice," *Handbook of*

Texas Online, accessed May 12, 2025, https://www.tshaonline. org/handbook/entries/tenayuca-emma-beatrice.

32. Rips, the *Texas Observer*, October 28, 1983.

33. Walker, 51,53.

34. Richard Croxdale, "Pecan-Shellers' Strike," *Handbook of Texas Online*, accessed May 13, 2025, https://www.tshaonline.org/ handbook/entries/pecan-shellers-strike.

35. Rips, the *Texas Observer*, October 28, 1983.

36. Rips, the *Texas Observer*, October 28, 1983. Note: Across historical records, the spelling of Tenayuca's nickname varies. I have chosen "La Pasionaria," the most common, but here, Lambert was quoted as saying "La Pasionara."

37. Richard Croxdale, "Pecan-Shellers' Strike," *Handbook of Texas Online*, accessed May 13, 2025, https://www.tshaonline.org/ handbook/entries/pecan-shellers-strike.

38. Mitchell, *Mean Things Happening In This Land*, 177.

39. Walker, 52.

40. Walker, 52.

41. Walker, 52.

42. Richard Croxdale, "Pecan-Shellers' Strike," *Handbook of Texas Online*, accessed May 13, 2025, https://www.tshaonline.org/ handbook/entries/pecan-shellers-strike.

43. Richard Croxdale, "Pecan-Shellers' Strike," *Handbook of Texas Online*

44. Richard Croxdale, "Pecan-Shellers' Strike," *Handbook of Texas Online*

45. Richard Croxdale, "Pecan-Shellers' Strike," *Handbook of Texas Online*

46. Walker, 52.

47. "Texas Talks Clip - Talking Tejano History: Emma Tenayuca." TSHA Online. October 24, 1992. Video, https://www.youtube. com/watch?v=htorlLAojk0.

48. Rips, the *Texas Observer*, October 28, 1983.

49. R. Matt Abigail and Jazmin León, "Tenayuca, Emma Beatrice," *Handbook of Texas Online*, accessed May 13, 2025, https://www.tshaonline.org/handbook/entries/tenayuca-emma-beatrice.

50. R. Matt Abigail and Jazmin León, "Tenayuca, Emma Beatrice," *Handbook of Texas Online*.

51. Rips, the *Texas Observer*, October 28, 1983.

Conclusion

1. Kaiser, Charles. "'We May Have Lost the South': What LBJ Really Said about Democrats in 1964." *The Guardian*, January 23, 2023. https://www.theguardian.com/books/2023/jan/22/we-may-have-lost-the-south-lbj-democrats-civil-rights-act-1964-bill-moyers.

2. "A Vote For Tower." *Texas Observer*, May 21, 1961. https://archives.texasobserver.org/issue/1961/05/20#page=1.

3. "A Vote For Tower." *Texas Observer*, May 21, 1961.

4. Roger M. Olien, "Oil and Gas Industry," *Handbook of Texas Online*, accessed November 11, 2025, https://www.tshaonline.org/handbook/entries/oil-and-gas-industry.

5. Wayne Thorburn, *Red State: An Insider's Story of How the GOP Came to Dominate Texas Politics* (University of Texas Press, 2014), 152.

6. James Moore and Wayne Slater, *Bush's Brain: How Karl Rove Made George W. Bush Presidential* (John Wiley & Sons, Inc., 2003) 67-68.

7. Patricia Kilday Hart. "It's Rick Perry's Party Now" *Texas Monthly*, October 2000. https://www.texasmonthly.com/news-politics/its-rick-perrys-party-now/

8.   Jan Reid, "Richards Sets a Politically Fateful Course on Guns." *The Texas Tribune.* October 4, 2012. https://www.texastribune. org/2012/10/04/richards-sets-politically-fateful-course-guns/.

9.   Patricia K. Hart, "Little Did We Know..." *Texas Monthly,* November 1, 2004. https://www.texasmonthly.com/news-politics/ little-did-we-know/.

10.   "Texas Job Loss During The NAFTA-WTO Period." *Citizen.Org. Public Citizen,* May 19, 2015. https://www.citizen.org/article/ texas-job-loss-during-the-nafta-wto-period/.

11.   Alex Birnel and David Griscom, "Texas's "Death Star Bill" Is an Attack on Workers and Democracy." *Jacobin,* June 24, 2023. https://jacobin.com/2023/06/texas-hb-2127-republican-party- minority-rule-workers-rights-democracy

12.   Cayla Harris and Benjamin Wermund, "Texas Democrats Lament Loss of National Party Investment as Midterms Begin." *Houston Chronicle,* October 31, 2022. https://www.houstonchronicle. com/politics/article/Texas-Democrats-lament-loss-of-national- party-17545359.php.

13.   Shane Goldmacher,. "How Kamala Harris Burned through $5 Billion in 15 Weeks." *The New York Times,* November 17, 2024. https://www.nytimes.com/2024/11/17/us/politics/harris- campaign-finances.html.

14.   Sam Russek,. "Inside the Rift between Texas Dems and a Soros- Backed PAC." The *Texas Observer.* October 8, 2025. https:// www.texasobserver.org/inside-rift-texas-democrats-soros- backed-pac/.

15.   Thorburn, *Red State,* 100-106.

16.   Clinton Willbanks & Michael E. Shepherd, "Texas in the Rear-View Mirror? How the Democratic Party Ignores Rural America and Underperforms in Elections" *Political Behavior* 24 May 2025. 11. https://link.springer.com/article/10.1007/s11109-025-10045- 3 https://doi.org/10.1007/s11109-025-10045-3. also see also:

Meagan Day, "Democrats Are Throwing in the Towel on Rural America." *Jacobin.* June 11, 2025. https://jacobin.com/2025/06/democrats-rural-america-elections-trump.

17. "Texas Exit Poll." *CNN*, March 3, 2020. https://www.cnn.com/election/2020/primaries-caucuses/entrance-and-exit-polls/texas/democratic.

18. *The Rebel,* September 9, 1911

19. Green, 307.

20. Matthew P. Rabbitt, Madeline Reed-Jones, Laura J. Hales, & Michael P. Burke, "Household food security in the United States in 2023" (Report No. ERR-337). *U.S. Department of Agriculture, Economic Research Service.* September, 2024. https://doi.org/10.32747/2024.8583175.ers

21. Pooja Salhotra,. "Texas's Statewide Poverty Rate Declines, but Several Rural Counties See Increase in Poor Residents." *Texas Tribune*, December 15, 2023. https://www.texastribune.org/2023/12/15/texas-poverty-rate-census-2022/.

22. Amanda Posson, Shannon Halbrook, and Samuel Cervantes. "Texas Is The Tale Of Two Economies." *Every Texan*. March 14, 2024. https://everytexan.org/2024/03/14/texas-is-the-tale-of-two-economies/.

23. Jeremy Wallace, "Why Greg Abbott Let Elon Musk Interrupt His Valentine's Day Dinner with His Wife." *Houston Chronicle*, April 5, 2025. https://www.houstonchronicle.com/politics/texas-take/article/musk-abbott-valentines-day-20257350.php.

24. Rips, the *Texas Observer*, October 28, 1983.

25. Juan Salinas II, and Elijah Nicholson-Messmer, "The Number of Texans in a Union Grew Slightly in 2023." *The Texas Tribune.* August 9, 2024. https://www.texastribune.org/2024/08/09/texas-union-member,ship-grows-2023/.

26. Emily Pontecorvo, "Why Texas Fossil Fuel Unions Signed on to This New Climate Plan." *Grist.* July 30, 2021. https://grist.org/climate-energy/why-texas-fossil-fuel-unions-signed-onto-a-climate-plan/.

27. Josh Peck, "Texas AFL-CIO Becomes First State Labor Federation to Call for Ceasefire in Gaza." *TPR.* January 30, 2024. https://www.tpr.org/government-politics/2024-01-30/texas-afl-cio-becomes-first-state-labor-federation-to-call-for-ceasefire-in-gaza.

28. Andrew Murray, "Jeremy Corbyn and the Battle for Socialism." *Jacobin*, February, 7, 2016. https://jacobin.com/2016/02/corbyn-socialism-labour-left-tony-benn-miliband.

29. Sam Gindin, "We Need a Politics That Is Not Only Class-Focused, but Class-Rooted." *Jacobin* August 22, 2020. https://jacobin.com/2020/08/politics-class-consciousness.

30. Gregg Cantrell, "The People's Revolt: Texas Populists and the Roots of American Liberalism," 424-437.

31. Eugene V. Debs, "Revolutionary Encampments," *National Rip-Saw*, September 1914, 12, https://www.marxists.org/history/usa/pubs/national-ripsaw/140900-nationalripsaw-v11n07w127.pdf.

32. Thomas Hickey Speech as transcribed in *The Rebel,* August 10, 1912.

33. Glen E. Lich, "Freethinkers," *Handbook of Texas Online*, accessed May 01, 2025, https://www.tshaonline.org/handbook/entries/freethinkers.

34. Stanley S. McGowen, "Battle or Massacre?: The Incident on the Nueces, August 10, 1862." *The Southwestern Historical Quarterly* 104, no. 1 (2000): 68. http://www.jstor.org/stable/30241669.

35. McGowen, "Battle or Massacre?," 69.

36. McGowen, "Battle or Massacre?," 76.

37. McGowen, "Battle or Massacre?," 77.

38. McGowen, "Battle or Massacre?," 77; Helen Thorpe, "Historical Friction," *Texas Monthly*, October 1997, https://www.texasmonthly.com/being-texan/historical-friction.

39. McGowen, "Battle or Massacre?," 78.

40. McGowen, "Battle or Massacre?," 78.

41. McGowen, "Battle or Massacre?," 78.

42. McGowen, 84.

43. McGowen, 80.

44. McGowen, 80.

45. Alter, 39.

46. "Battle of the Nueces," *Handbook of Texas Online*, accessed May 01, 2025, https://www.tshaonline.org/handbook/entries/nueces-battle-of-the.

© Bobby Scheidemann

David Griscom is a writer and political commentator with a focus on working-class politics and history, especially in the South and Texas. His work on Southern labor history can be found in *Jacobin*. David is also the host of The Jacobin Show and co-host of the podcast Left Reckoning. Formerly a producer on The Michael Brooks Show, he now lives in his hometown of Austin, Texas.

Subscribe to the OR Books Mailing List
and get 30% off your first order at
www.orbooks.com